CONTENTS

[5]

PREFACE

The *Hobart Papers* are intended to contribute a stream of authoritative, independent and lucid analyses to the understanding and application of economics to private and government activity. Their characteristic theme has been the optimum use of scarce resources and the extent to which it can best be achieved in markets within an appropriate framework of laws and institutions or, where markets cannot work or have disproportionate defects, by better methods with relative advantages or less decisive defects. Since the alternative to the market is in practice the state, and both are imperfect, the choice between them is effectively made on the judgement of the comparative consequences of 'market failure' and 'government failure'.

The concentration of economists in post-war years until recently on macro-economic management of the economy and on macro-models distracted attention from the fruitfulness of micro-economic analysis in examining the conditions in which individual commodities or services were supplied, and the problems encountered in meeting the preferences and requirements of the consumer. In contrast to the prevailing preoccupation with macro-economics, the Institute sponsored studies of subjects for which macro-economic analysis would have been irrelevant or abortive. These subjects were largely neglected in the economic text-books, and it may have come to be thought that economics had little light to shed on them; academic writing on them was either non-existent or was the work of sociologists or social administrators who largely missed the economic essentials. Social science departments in British universities still do not always teach their students economic analysis, without which their subject can be barren.

The Institute has published such micro-economic studies in the 'welfare' services—pensions (1957, 1960), housing (1960), health (1961 onwards), on libraries (1962), television (1962, 1968), education (1963), parking (1965), roads (1966), fire services (1967), nuclear power (1967), blood (1968), art and antiques (1969), animal semen (1972), aircraft (1974), police (1974), pollution property rights (1975), and more.

Hobart Paper 79 is a study in the application of market analysis to bread. The author, Dr W. Duncan Reekie of

[7]

Edinburgh University, writes as an independent analyst but with knowledge of the industry, beginning with personal experience of working in it, and as a student of its history. He has written a unique study not available in any comparable form in British economic writing. He analyses the conditions of the supply of bread and the demand for it and the nature of the resulting pricing processes. He examines the structure of the industry comprising small and large millers and bakers, sometimes integrated, and the structure of consumer tastes and preferences. Not least he examines the attempts by government for seven centuries to control the weight and/or price of bread, from the Assize of Bread and Ale in 1266 to the price-fixing of Mrs Shirley Williams and Mr Roy Hattersley in 1977-78— all, of course, 'in the public interest'. Not infrequently they set out to help the consumer by regulating weight and price and ended by harming him (or rather her) by suppressing competition. And trade unions have been no better.

Dr Reekie's study is thus not only of the economics of bread production for a market but of the political economy of government regulation. And his main conclusion is that the consumer has been frustrated not by the capacity of the producers to exploit him (or rather her) but by the incapacity of politicians to understand the consequences of their good (or bad) intentions.

The *Paper* ranges deep into the nature of the supply of bread and the demand for it and wide over several centuries up to the latest attempts of government to regulate the price of bread in recent months. It shows that the market would have worked much better if government had not damaged it. The consumer was harmed not by producer monopoly but by government regulation.

Dr Reekie has written a scholarly, informed and austerely objective study of the staple of British diet. It is an outstanding example of the fruitful application of market analysis, and it leads the author to conclusions about the waywardness of government regulation. It is thus a compound of technical economic theory and of the economics of politics. It should be of interest not only to teachers and students of economics but also to students of government and of its indifferent record down the centuries.

The Institute's constitution requires it to dissociate its Trustees, Directors and Advisers from the analysis and recommendations of its authors. It wishes to thank Professor Basil S. Yamey of the London School of Economics and Professor Dennis Lees of Nottingham University for reading early drafts and for offering comments and suggestions that the author has borne in mind in his final revisions. Dr Reekie's text is a notable contribution to the *Hobart Papers*.

February 1978   ARTHUR SELDON

THE AUTHOR

W. DUNCAN REEKIE graduated BCom (with Distinction) from Edinburgh University in 1963. From 1963 to 1966 he worked in an independent bakery firm later absorbed by a leading biscuit manufacturer. He obtained his PhD in economics at the University of Strathclyde in 1969. He is a specialist in the economics of industrial organisation, has held teaching posts in the University of the Witwatersrand, Johannesburg, and, as Associate Professor, in the University of Toronto. He now holds a lectureship in Business Studies in the University of Edinburgh. His books include *Advertising* (1974), *The Economics of the Pharmaceutical Industry* (1975), and *Managerial Economics* (1975). He has contributed to the professional periodicals, including *The Economic Journal, The Scottish Journal of Political Economy, Applied Economics,* and *The Journal of Industrial Economics.*

ACKNOWLEDGEMENTS

This *Paper* has benefited from the comments or discussion of Professor Hilde Behrend, Paul Charlton, David Dodds, Dr I. R. C. Hirst, Professor N. C. Hunt, Harold Lind, Dr I. H. N. McNicholl, and Garry Weston. The editorial advice of Arthur Seldon was constructive and fastidious. Mr Seldon has helped improve both my analysis and my style. All remaining defects are attributable solely to me.

November 1977   W.D.R.

I. INTRODUCTION

Bread was probably first made in the Neolithic era, some 12,000 years ago. The dough was made of coarsely crushed grain mixed with water, dried in the sun or laid on stones and baked by covering with hot ashes. Baking is one of the oldest and most important of all industries. Bread, until recently, was the major and sometimes the sole source of manufactured food for the bulk of the population. It is a long established but now declining industry.

Governments have been made or broken by the price of bread. Regulatory control of the industry consequently has a long and complex history. The Assize of Bread in 1266 introduced rules governing the weight and sale of the product, and were in force in an amended form until the beginning of the 19th century. The debates on the passing and repeal of the Corn Laws represented major milestones in British political and economic thought. In the 20th century British bread has been subject to price controls, ingredient controls, advertising controls, subsidies and rationing. A plethora of government bodies have investigated the industry and made recommendations.

(i) *The immediate issue*

Government intervention in the bread industry is said to be essential. Mr Roy Hattersley, the Secretary of State for Prices and Consumer Protection, expressed this view emphatically in the House of Commons in December 1976:

> 'Were it possible for the government to withdraw from involvement in the baking and bread distribution industry I would certainly choose to do so. I am, however, convinced that our complete withdrawal would prejudice the interests of consumers, bakers and small retailers.'[1]

Control of the bread industry is, apparently in the public interest.

This view went unchallenged in the examination of the industry by the Monopolies and Mergers Commission,[2] which discovered two main non-competitive conditions. First, each major milling group requires its flour-using subsidiaries to buy flour from its mills (para. 463). Since this practice permitted

---

[1] *Trade and Industry,* 17 December, 1976.

[2] Monopolies and Mergers Commission, *Flour and Bread,* HC 412, HMSO, 1977.

economies of scale and specialisation, and since the millers did not discriminate in price between their own subsidiaries and external customers, it was deemed not to be against the public interest (paras. 491-2). Second, the Commission found that the leading bread firms had in the period 1970 to 1974 entered into restrictive agreements limiting the discounts which could be passed on to bread retailers (para. 483). It was this discovery which encouraged Mr Gordon Borrie, the Director General of the Office of Fair Trading, to ask the government 'to give him more powers to stamp out secret restricted trading agreements and price rings'.[1] The Commission, however, conceded that the agreements were 'not notably successful because . . . of the mutual distrust which existed between the major bakery groups' (para. 291).

Lack of profitability in baking—government controls

The Commission also revealed that the three largest baking firms, Associated British Foods Ltd. (ABF), Ranks Hovis McDougall Ltd. (RHM), and Spillers Ltd., had been making losses on their bread-baking activities for several successive years (para. 396). The Commission attributed their unprofitability 'largely to the effects of statutory price control and other forms of official intervention' (para. 504). The firms found it possible to continue in business as bakers as a consequence of the increasing profitability of their flour-milling (Table I). The industry was thus given a clean bill of health and the impact on competition of existing controls (outside the Commission's jurisdiction) was subject to mainly inconclusive consideration (paras. 295-307).

Disparity between milling and baking profits is not new. Millers have generally enjoyed a higher degree of bargaining power than bakers. But, the Commission said,

'On its present scale [it] is to a considerable extent the result of distorting effects of statutory controls . . . [which] have depressed bread prices much more severely than flour prices' (para. 495).

For political reasons, it has been easier for millers to obtain permission from government to raise flour prices than it has been for bakers to raise bread prices.[2] An unprofitable bread

---

[1] *The Times*, 17 March, 1977.

[2] Flour is sold to bakers whose votes are few. Bread is sold to housewives who form a large part of the electorate. 'The Median Voter Theorem' is discussed in Gordon Tullock, *The Vote Motive*, Hobart Paperback No. 9, IEA, 1976, p. 14.

Give Us This Day . . .
W. DUNCAN REEKIE

1. The three largest bread firms have made losses as a deliberate consequence of government policies. Their continued existence has been possible only by cross-subsidisation from their profitable flour-milling activities.

2. For political reasons controls on the price of bread have been stricter and more complex than those on the price of flour.

3. The industry's main product is the homogeneous standard loaf. Uniformity has been imposed by government decree. Standardisation continues to be approved of and encouraged by government.

4. Price competition has frequently been suppressed by government decree, most recently in 1974-76. The outcome has been higher prices for consumers.

5. Many baking and milling firms are not averse to co-operating with government, ostensibly in the consumer interest, but with outcomes which primarily benefit themselves.

6. Trade union action depriving consumers of lower prices has been allowed by government by default.

7. Government controls have not kept the price of bread low.

8. There are neither welfare nor macro-economic management reasons why government should have a close involvement with the bread industry.

9. New or existing bread bakers and distributors have continually sought for new and improved ways of providing the housewife with the product she wants at the price she is prepared to pay.

10. The 1977 Monopolies Commission investigation failed both to detail the benefits competition has brought to the consumer and to condemn the disadvantages of government-inspired suppression of competition. Its Report thus failed to uphold the Fair Trading Act of 1973 which stated that the public interest is best served through competition.

11. There is no evidence that a vertically-integrated milling and baking industry is the most efficient form of industrial organisation. Cross-subsidisation of baking by milling is incited by legislation. Consumer preferences are swinging towards non-standardised, higher-priced products (of in-store bakeries or the hot-bread shops, etc.) where entry is easy and vertical integration not essential. Competition would thus intensify spontaneously if not distorted by government.

12. It is not monopoly but government efforts to regulate the industry that has damaged the consumer interest.

Hobart Paper 79 is published price (£1·20) by

THE INSTITUTE OF ECONOMIC AFFAIRS
2 Lord North Street, Westminster
London SW1P 3LB   Telephone: 01-799 3745

IEA PUBLICATIONS

Subscription Service

An annual subscription is the most convenient way to obtain our publications. Every title we produce in our regular series will be sent to you immediately on publication and without further charge, representing a substantial saving.

Subscription rates

Britain: £10.00 p.a. including postage, reduced to £9.50 p.a. if paid by Banker's Order.

£7.50 p.a. to students and also to teachers who pay *personally.* No reduction for Banker's Orders.

Europe: 30 US dollars or equivalent.

North America: 35 US dollars.

Other countries: Rates on application. In many countries subscriptions are handled by local agents.

These rates are *not* available to companies or to institutions.

....

To: The Treasurer,
    Institute of Economic Affairs,
    2 Lord North Street,
    Westminster, London SW1P 3LB.

I should like an individual subscription beginning ....

I enclose a cheque/postal order for:

☐ £10.00
☐ £7.50 [student/teacher at ....]
☐ Please send me a Banker's Order form
☐ Please send me an Invoice

Name...

Address ....

        ....

Signed.. Date.................

HP79

TABLE I

RETURN ON CAPITAL EMPLOYED IN FLOUR MILLING AND BREAD BAKING, 1971-75

(per cent)

Historic cost basis	*1971*	*1972*	*1973*	*1974*	*1975*
ABF					
Flour milling	36·9	38·2	29·7	53·0	56·3
Bread baking	10·0	6·9	loss	loss	loss
Flour milling and bread baking	19·5	17·6	5·9	11·2	19·9
RHM					
Flour milling	17·6	14·4	23·0	26·0	32·4
Bread baking	15·7	16·7	6·2	loss	loss
Flour milling and bread baking	16·7	15·5	15·8	11·5	17·2
SPILLERS					
Flour milling	n.a.	13·0	18·1	27·8	32·2
Bread baking	n.a.	loss	loss	loss	loss
Flour milling and bread baking	—	4·0	0·9	6·4	18·2
UK Manufacturing Industry	12·5	15·0	17·4	17·0	15·2

Source: Flour and Bread, HC 412, para. 396.

industry is a deliberate consequence of government policies.

The corollary is that vertical integration has been further encouraged to permit cross-subsidisation, and some independent plant bakers have been forced to leave the industry (para. 296). Since this exodus was 'not attributable to anything done by the three major groups' (para. 504), the Commission did not consider it fell within its remit to appraise its effects on the public interest.

Similarly the Commission did not comment on the restrictive price and advertising agreements entered into by the leading three firms *'At the suggestion of Government'* (para. 300) (my italics). These restrictive practices inhibited price competition by independent bakers but did not draw criticism from either the Commission or the Office of Fair Trading.

The immediate question is whether the thinking of the Monopolies Commission conflicts with statutory competition policy. The inquiry was carried out under the terms of the 1948 Monopolies Act.[1] This Act was notoriously vague about the criteria to be used in judging how the public interest is affected by monopolistic conduct or structure.[2] This very vagueness, however, embodied sufficient pragmatism to enable the Commission to apply the economically more specific yardsticks of the 1973 Fair Trading Act had it so wished. Among other things, Clause 84 of the 1973 Act enjoins the Commission to maintain and promote competition and new entry in order to reduce costs and encourage innovation.[3]

Are the conclusions of the Report on the bread industry consistent with the spirit of both the 1948 and 1973 Acts? This *Paper* suggests they merely comply with the ambiguous 1948 Act. Have the government's other controls fostered entry and competition? This *Paper* suggests they have reduced competition and encouraged exit from the industry.

(ii) *The wider issue*

How does all this affect the industry's performance in providing the consumer with the quantity and quality of bread she wants at the price she is willing to pay?

The chief contentions we will examine are briefly that

(i) there are strong 'social' reasons for controlling the bread industry;

(ii) without some authoritative source of guidance, efficient and satisfactory bread production and distribution would not be obtained;

(iii) the industry has an unnecessary proliferation of products;

(iv) there is needless duplication of distribution systems;

(v) the market power of the leading bakers and millers is excessive and is abused;

---

[1] As the reference was made before the commencement of the 1973 Act it was conducted as though earlier Acts had not been repealed.

[2] Professor G. C. Allen (a former member of the Commission) wrote in *Monopoly and Restrictive Practices*, Allen & Unwin, 1968, pp. 66: '. . . the guidance given by the Act consisted of a string of platitudes which the Commission found valueless, and it was left for the members themselves to reach their own conclusions by reference to the assumptions, principles or prejudices which their training and experience caused them to apply to economic affairs'.

[3] These are all subject to a general requirement that the Commission also takes everything into account which it thinks relevant. The 1973 Act is still open-ended.

(vi) the industry is inefficient in its use of labour and equipment.

A critical examination of these issues requires knowledge of some of the economic history of the industry. After presenting the relevant background and analysing the economics of the industry, the *Paper* proposes a programme for reform which aims to ensure for consumers an efficient supply of bread of the desired quantity and quality.

II. A HISTORY OF THE INDUSTRY

The characteristics and texture of bread have been basically unchanged for thousands of years, and the raw materials—yeast, flour and water—have likewise remained the same.

(i) *Technological developments*

Today most flour is milled in steel roller mills. Millstones are retained for only a few speciality flours. Messrs R. Shepphard and E. Newton,[1] bread industry historians, regarded the roller mill as the most significant technological advance in the industry since the addition of yeast to the ingredient mix 4,000 years previously. The first British roller mill was built in Glasgow in 1872[2] and by 1910 some three-quarters of the country's water- and wind-mills had become derelict.

Roller mills were originally powered by steam and led to low-cost production of flour generally. In particular, they permitted the easy separation of the complete wheatgerm, and so produced finer, more consistent and whiter flour.

Baking techniques too have changed little since the origins of bread, although the procedures have become increasingly mechanised. The ingredients are kneaded into a dough, divided into the appropriate sizes of portion and 'proved' (aerated by the action of yeast) before baking. Man-handling of bulky raw materials in the bakery can now be replaced by mechanised elevators. Mechanical mixers, dividers and moulders have been developed and, in modern larger-scale plants, they now operate on largely automatic or computer-controlled principles. The bakers' oven, heated by coal or coke, remained of the simplest design until last century. They were loaded with a long-handled wooden 'peel' with which the ovenman placed

---

[1] *The Story of Bread*, Routledge and Kegan Paul, 1957, p. 4.

[2] *Ibid.*, p. 10: the roller mill, with iron rollers, was invented in Switzerland in 1834.

the baking tins swiftly and precisely into the appropriate part of the oven. This cumbersome and lengthy process was overcome by the invention of the draw-plate oven whereby the bottom plate, mounted on wheels, is withdrawn completely from the baking chamber. Loading and unloading can be performed in one operation. Gas and oil have replaced solid fuels for heating most ovens and completely for the most advanced, the long-heated travelling oven, developed at the turn of the century, through which bread passes slowly on a moving conveyer emerging baked at the far end.

Other major developments which had particularly important implications for the industry were slicing and wrapping machines and the road transport revolution of the 1920s and 1930s. Together they widened the potential market of the baker geographically and in type of outlet. No longer was he limited to selling in a shop *in situ* with the bakery.

(ii) *Organisational changes in supply*

The bakery trade existed in London as early as the 11th century.[1] But in non-metropolitan areas baking was carried out either domestically or in communal ovens: '. . . even in 1804, Manchester with a population of 100,000 had no commercial bakers'.[2] The importance of bread in the family budget, the relative poverty of the population, and the apparent immoral luxury of using a merchant baker can be deduced from what William Cobbett wrote in 1821:[3]

> 'How wasteful, and indeed how shameful for a labourer's wife to go to the baker's shop; and how negligent and how criminally careless of the welfare of his family must the labourer be who permits so scandalous a use of the proceeds of his labour.'

By 1850 there were some 50,000[4] bakers in towns; almost all baked and sold on the premises. In the 20th century economies of scale in manufacture and distribution resulted in substantial changes in this structure. The cost-saving technological advances encouraged larger-scale plants; and the constraint of perishability was overcome by road transport. Plant bakeries,

---

[1] P. Maunder, *The Bread Industry in the United Kingdom,* Universities of Nottingham and Loughborough, 1970, p. 12.

[2] Shepphard and Newton, *op. cit.,* p. 31.

[3] Cited *ibid.,* p. 29. Cobbett, apparently, had still not learned of the advantages of Adam Smith's principle of the division of labour.

[4] Maunder, *op. cit.,* p. 12.

TABLE II

NUMBER OF MULTIPLE-SHOP BREAD FIRMS AND BRANCHES OF FIRMS WITH 10 OR MORE BRANCHES, 1900-50

	No. of Firms	No. of Branches
1900	11	265
1910	25	782
1920	40	1,237
1930	82	1,820
1939	79	2,390
1950	69	2,659

Source: J. B. Jeffreys, 'The Bread and Flour Confectionery Trade', in *Retail Trading in Britain, 1850-1950*, Cambridge for the NIESR, 1955, p. 214.

in which production is largely automatic and which supply a multiplicity of outlets, grew in number; the traditional master baker declined. At the turn of the century there were a mere handful of plant bakeries. By 1950 the number of branch shops serviced by central plants had increased ten-fold to over 2,500 (Table II).

This rise in the number of plants intensified local competition. Consumer choice was widened in towns and villages previously supplied by oligopolies or monopolies[1] of master bakers. In addition, plant bakers sold through grocers, dairies and general stores. The range of alternative sources of supply of bread for the consumer was increased. Bought bread no longer had to be purchased at the baker's shop. By 1938 Jeffreys noted that 22-26 per cent of *plant*-produced bread passed through outlets not owned by the plants,[2] and by 1965 this figure had risen to around 60 per cent.[3]

The competitive process was also operating to curb any market power the plant bakers might acquire. The well-known group of retail outlets of J. Lyons and Co. Ltd. integrated backwards[4] into bread production before 1939 and by the

[1] Markets supplied by only a few sellers are oligopolies, by a single seller monopoly.

[2] Jeffreys, *op. cit.*, p. 167.

[3] National Board for Prices and Incomes, *Prices of Bread and Flour*, Report No. 3, Cmnd. 2760, HMSO, 1965, para. 13, p. 3.

[4] Backward integration indicates that the firm was now undertaking an activity in the productive process one or more stages removed from the final consumer. Forward integration occurs when the firm undertakes activities in the chain of production closer to the final market.

1950s had become a major producer. Others, such as the pioneer grocery chains of Home & Colonial, Maypole and Liptons, used their bargaining power to counter that of the plant bakers and so could often use bread as a 'loss leader'.[1]

Integration and competition in milling

Meanwhile in flour milling the scale and quality advantages of the roller mill encouraged the emergence of larger mills and fewer milling firms. By 1935 there were only 2,600 millers in Britain and three firms (Ranks, Spillers and the Co-operative Wholesale Society) controlled 39 per cent of the output of flour. By 1944 the percentage had risen to 66 per cent as a consequence of mergers and rationalisation into fewer units. This led the Prices and Incomes Board to remark:

> 'Time was when a few milling groups, selling flour to an army of small and medium-sized bakers, enjoyed an apparently unassailable bargaining advantage . . . reflected . . . in a traditionally high return on investment in flour milling and a traditionally low return on investment in baking.'[2]

Again the competitive process operated to redress the balance of bargaining power. Mr Garfield Weston acquired a number of regional bakeries which continued to trade under their own names as subsidiaries of his Allied Bakeries. This began in 1935, was halted by war, but by 1954 Allied owned 72 bakery plants and 642 shops. Ranks and Spillers both refused to give Allied special discounts. However, the decontrol of the grain trade in 1953 again allowed bakers, by law, to use imported flour. Allied Bakeries promptly imported cheaper flour from Canada, and later Australia, blending the imports with English flour. Other bakery firms followed Weston's example and the domestic millers found it necessary to close mills and put others on short-time working. Eventually price concessions were given but too late for the millers to maintain their market leadership. Allied began to integrate backwards; and by 1962 it had acquired 29 millers and had significantly reduced its reliance on imports.[3]

The rivalry between Allied and the three main millers produced predictable retaliation. Forward integration into baking occurred as the millers attempted to secure their markets for flour in the face of a declining total demand. The

---

[1] Maunder, *op. cit.*, p. 49.   [2] Cmnd. 2760, para. 12.   [3] Maunder, *op. cit.*, p. 25.

mid-1950s saw the start of a sellers' market for master bakers and 'large sums were paid for the goodwill'[1] of small firms. Most acquisitions were kept secret for as long as possible and the acquired companies generally continued to trade under their original name and to manufacture other bakery products, if not bread, in their original premises. Not until the 1960s did company annual reports begin to reveal the full extent of the millers' bakery interests.

In 1962 Ranks merged with Hovis McDougall to form RHM Ltd. In the same year its bakery subsidiary, British Bakeries Ltd., acquired 72 firms and, in 1964, 78 other subsidiaries.[2] Between 1954 and 1976 over 700 production or distribution firms had been purchased by RHM for an outlay of some £33 million.[3]

In the Co-operative movement, more and more retail societies stopped baking and groups of societies established federal plant bakeries. The CWS, which was experiencing falling flour sales due to poor performance by retail co-operatives, encouraged this trend, and in 1958 took a 50 per cent interest in all federal bakeries. It then proceeded to acquire complete control of federals and by 1971 only three federals and nine retail bread bakeries were still independent. In 1970 the CWS merged its bread interests with those of Lyons, and in 1971 Spillers merged its bakery interests with CWS-Lyons to become comparable in size to RHM and ABF.[4]

The impact of this forward and backward integration, coupled with mergers at the same stage of the productive process, can be put into numerical perspective. Messrs H. Leak and A. Maizels estimated[5] that in 1935 there were 24,000 bakers and confectioners in the country, but that only 40 of them had over 500 employees. The industry fell into the 'Low Concentration' category. The net output of the top three firms was 10 per cent of the total. In terms of bread alone, and classifying the industry by organisation type, in 1938 plant bakers held 24-26 per cent of consumer expenditure on bread,

[1] *Ibid.*, p. 23.

[2] P. E. Hart, M. A. Utton and G. Walshe, *Mergers and Concentration in British Industry*, Cambridge, 1973, p. 49.

[3] HC 412, para. 156.

[4] Hart, Utton and Walshe, *op. cit.*, p. 49.

[5] 'The Structure of British Industry', *Journal of the Royal Statistical Society*, Vol. CVIII, Parts I-II, 1945, pp.142-99.

TABLE III

NUMBERS OF SMALL AND LARGE ESTABLISHMENTS AND NUMBERS EMPLOYED, 1935 AND 1951

	1935	1951	% Change
Numbers of establishments with			
11 or more employees	2,650	1,900	−28
Numbers employed	105,000	132,000	+25
Numbers of establishments with			
10 or fewer employees	20,900	13,200	−36
Numbers employed	78,000	60,000	−23

Source: Census of Production, 1935 and 1951.

TABLE IV

CONCENTRATION IN THE BREAD AND FLOUR CONFECTIONERY INDUSTRY, 1963

(Five-firm concentration ratio = 71·4%)

Size of Establishments and Enterprises (1963)

	Establishments		Enterprises	
No. of Employees	No.	% of Employees	No.	% of Employees
Under 100	1,099	15	862	10
100-749	377	61	122	17
750-1,499	25	16	10	7
1,500 and over	6	8	9	66
	1,507	100	1,003	100

Source: C. F. Pratten, *Economies of Scale in Manufacturing Industry*, Cambridge, 1971, p. 77.

master bakers 53-57 per cent and retail co-operatives or federal bakeries owned by them 19-21 per cent.[1]

Messrs R. W. Evely and I. M. D. Little argued[2] that the growth of Allied Bakeries 'probably accounted . . . for the greater part of the increase in the trade's concentration from 1935 to 1951'. The numbers employed in large establishments rose by 25 per cent over that period, and fell by a similar percentage in small establishments (Table III).

[1] Maunder, *op. cit.*, p.14.

[2] *Concentration in British Industry*, Cambridge, 1960, p. 259.

[20]

TABLE V

BREAD: PRODUCTION SHARES OF LEADING FIRMS, 1965-75, AND NUMBERS OF BREAD BAKERIES, 1975-76

	Production Share						*No.*
	1965	*1967*	*1969*	*1971*	*1973*	*1975*	*of Bakeries*
	%	%	%	%	%	%	
SPILLERS	10·7	11·1	11·0	11·1	17·2	16·5	36 (1976)
RHM	21·1	23·3	23·7	23·9	25·2	23·3	83 (1975)
ABF	19·4	16·9	17·9	17·0	20·6	21·7	43 (1975)
	51·2	50·3	52·6	52·0	63·0	61·5	162

Source: HC 412, *op. cit.,* paras. 138, 169, 193 and 280.

Table IV, while not restricted to the bread industry, illustrates how, although 73 per cent of all employees work for larger firms, 76 per cent of them work in smaller establishments. The bread industry is now concentrated in terms of ownership, but remains fragmented in numbers of plants (Tables IV and V). The main reasons for the continuing existence of large numbers of bakeries are the perishability of the product and its high transport costs relative to value.

(iii) *The trend of demand*

Bread is an 'inferior good': less of it is purchased by consumers with higher incomes.[1] This is true both over time, as consumer incomes and the general standard of living have risen, and at a point in time between the consumption patterns of richer and poorer people.

Between 1954 and 1974 UK flour consumption fell from 4,314,000 tons to 3,635,000 tons per annum, a 16 per cent decrease. Because of a rising population this fall is even steeper if calculated on an individual basis: consumption per head fell from 187·2 lbs to 135·5 lbs, a drop of 28 per cent (Table VI). Flour, however, is an ingredient in products other than bread, many of which can be regarded as luxuries rather than staples. The second part of Table VI is restricted to bread consumption in Great Britain and depicts a drop in consumption of 22·8 oz per head per week between 1954 and 1974, a reduction in

[1] Less is bought because people prefer, as they become better off, to spend relatively more on 'luxury' goods and absolutely less on bread.

TABLE VI

TOTAL FLOUR CONSUMPTION: UNITED KINGDOM, 1949-74; AND HOUSEHOLD BREAD CONSUMPTION: GREAT BRITAIN, 1952-74

	FLOUR		BREAD
	000 tons	*lbs per head per year*	*Ounces per person per week*
1949	5,084	222·2	—
1952	4,674	201·7	61·46
1955	4,223	182·5	55·13
1958	4,045	171·5	47·21
1961	3,964	164·0	45·17
1964	3,856	156·0	41·97
1967	3,746	147·0	40·02
1970	3,783	145·2	38·11
1973	3,721	140·3	33·42
1974	3,635	135·5	33·5

Sources: Flour: *Annual Abstracts of Statistics,* HMSO.

Bread: Ministry of Agriculture, Fisheries and Food, *Household Food Consumption and Expenditure* (Annual Reports of the National Food Survey Committee: 1964-75), HMSO.

demand of 40 per cent. Flour is a declining industry in the UK, and the bread industry, the overwhelmingly dominant outlet for flour, has been declining at an even faster rate.

This decline is no new phenomenon. In 1880 annual flour consumption was around 280 lb per head. By the outbreak of World War I it was down to 211 lb. The general rise in the standard of living has been accompanied by both a wider range and availability of convenience and luxury foods. The National Food Survey (from which Table VII is abstracted) does not cover bread consumed outside the home (in canteens, cafés, restaurants, pubs, etc.) where demand tends to have risen over the past few years. So the total decline is not so marked as the available data suggest.[1]

Table VII also indicates that richer families (groups A and B) consumed less bread per head than the average household in 1955 and 1973, and poorer families (groups C and D) consumed more.[2] By 1973 the general decline in bread consump-

[1] 11 per cent of total production goes to the catering trade: Economist Intelligence Unit, *Retail Business*, Report No. 220, 1976.

[2] In technical language, income elasticity of demand was negative.

TABLE VII

BREAD: WEEKLY CONSUMPTION PER PERSON, BY INCOME GROUP, 1955 AND 1973

Income Group	1955 Oz per Week	Index	1973 Oz per Week	Index
D1	59·7	108·29	38·88	116·34
C	58·56	106·22	36·75	109·96
B	53·75	97·5	32·64	97·66
A	46·74	84·78	26·43	79·08
All households	55·13	100·0	33·42	100·0

Note: In 1955, D1, C, B and A groupings refer to gross weekly head of household incomes of under £6, £6 to under £9, £9 to under £15, and £15 and over respectively. In 1973 the corresponding boundaries used were £19·50, £34 and £60 respectively.

Source: Ministry of Agriculture, Fisheries and Food, *Household Food Consumption and Expenditure* (Annual Reports of the National Food Survey Committee).

tion had apparently proceeded faster among group A consumers. In relation to total family income or expenditure the differentials are interesting rather than significant. Undoubtedly there were times before or shortly after the last war when a rise in the price of bread could inflict hardship on a poorer family. Today bread price movements have a much smaller effect on the Cost of Living Index than 20 or even 10 years ago. For instance, out of the 1,000 points comprising the Index in 1975 only 12 were allocated to bread compared with 27 in 1955. The change in the weighting given to bread in the Index is supported by the evidence of declining consumption in Table VII.

Table VIII shows how bread consumption is dominated by the large white standard loaf and, in particular, by the sliced wrapped loaf. The figures show no marked change in the public's preference between brown and white bread over the last few years. Industry spokesmen regard figures such as these as indicating 'clearly how the public, with complete freedom of choice, has an overwhelming preference for the large white sliced wrapped loaf'.[1] I suggest there is an alternative and opposite view: it accepts that consumer preferences favour the standard loaf over the available alternatives but contends that a combination of the current regulatory environment and the

[1] Cited from *Facts about Bread*, Flour Advisory Bureau, 1975, p. 15.

TABLE VIII

ESTIMATED HOUSEHOLD CONSUMPTION OF BREAD BY TYPE, 1968 AND 1973

(oz per person per week)

	1968	%	1973	%
Brown	2·63	6·8	2·22	6·6
Wholewheat/meal	0·42	1·1	0·54	1·6
White large unwrapped	6·38	16·6	6·19	18·5
White large wrapped	21·14	55·3	17·56	52·5
White small unwrapped	2·97	7·7	2·50	7·4
White small wrapped	1·82	4·8	1·33	3·9
Others*	2·95	7·7	3·08	9·2
	38·31		33·42	

* Malt bread, fruit bread, French bread, milk bread, 'slimming' bread, white and brown bread rolls.

Source: *Household Food Consumption and Expenditure* (Annual Reports of the National Food Survey Committee), *op. cit.*

oligopolistic structure of the industry has resulted in an effective *restriction* of consumer choice.

(iv) *Regulatory background*

The Assize of Bread, 1266

To understand the latter contention, the real or supposed regulations which govern the industry's competitive behaviour must be examined. They can be traced back to the 1266 Assize of Bread and Ale, a comprehensive law which strictly controlled the baking and selling of bread.[1] Lengthy numerical tables showed how the weight of the loaf should be reduced for every rise in the price of wheat. It was enacted in a century when there had been a succession of bad harvests. While the peasantry and other common people starved, the nobility and higher ranks of the clergy continued to feast conspicuously. Bread, the staff of life, was priced, because of scarcity, beyond the reach of the populace. The rules of 1266, which lasted for over five centuries, were nominally meant to change this situation. They were laid down

[1] A much simpler, less comprehensive law had been in existence since the first (1202) Assize of Bread. Both it and the 1266 Assize attempted to embody the then current notion of what a 'just' or 'reasonable' price should be.

[24]

'for fear of revolution, rather than any real concern for the welfare of the people . . . But while [they] succeeded in keeping down the price of the loaf [they] could not prevent shortage'.[1]

The Assize tables started with wheat at 6d per quarter, ended at £5 and were computed for four types of bread (in descending order of quality and ascending order of weight): halfpenny white, penny white, penny wheaten and penny household. The tables were calculated to provide the baker with a given profit, from costs arrived at from official test-bakes. Predictably, the bakers felt that test-bakes were conducted too infrequently to account for rising costs (other than wheat) and that inadequate recognition was given to their overhead costs. In 1303 an allowance of $\frac{1}{2}$d was added to cover the costs of a dog and later the London Bakers' Company successfully lobbied for the allowance to cover not only wood, candles, journeymen and apprentices, salt, yeast, and the millers' charges, but also the costs of the baker's house, a cat and even a wife.[2]

The statutory allowance was abandoned in 1709. Magistrates, whose duty had been to decide the weight of the loaf according to the Assize tables, were then also given discretion in fixing the allowance. This power resulted in a number of bakers being placed in serious financial difficulties due to variations in treatment by magistrates of different bakers. The situation continued to deteriorate when discretion was further increased to allow magistrates to set the Assize from the price of either wheat or flour. Since flour prices and qualities varied between mills, customers' localities and over time, it was not surprising that members of the trade were financially very unhappy by the end of the 18th century.

Meanwhile, millers were subject to little or no control. Continuous petitioning of Parliament by the bakers went on and the authorities began to feel the Assize laws were more trouble than they were worth. The uniform, regulated price of bread kept high-cost inefficient traders in existence by protecting them from price competition. Expansion by efficient bakers who could cut prices was precluded when the regulated price was relatively high. Conversely, traders who were too small to obtain bulk discounts from the miller, or whose purchases of flour were made at a time or place of high prices or low quality, were at a

---

[1] Shepphard and Newton, *op. cit.*, p. 48.

[2] *Ibid.*, p. 50.

[25]

disadvantage compared to their fellows when the fixed price of bread was relatively low. In 1795 the London Bakers' Company was told by the Prime Minister, William Pitt, 'Gentlemen . . . you shall have relief'.[1] 'Relief' took two more years to arrive and took the form of an increase in the bakers' allowance and a revision of the method of computation. The magistrates began to work on an average flour price determined from records of purchases made and prices paid by each baker instead of on arbitrary reports of flour prices gleaned from haphazard checks of the markets. The system was not dissimilar from that operated by the Ministry of Agriculture, Fisheries and Food in the 1950s.

Repeal of the Assize of Bread, 1815

The authorities began to discuss the possibility of decontrol. But at the first talk of freedom of trade the bakers did an abrupt *volte face*. The London Bakers' Company, in evidence to a parliamentary committee in the early 1800s, argued that under free competition the baker with capital would have an unfair advantage.[2] He would be better able to survive bad harvests than his smaller neighbour, would monopolise the trade and then raise prices excessively in times of wheat shortage. It 'was the old story of the least efficient and progressive hankering after the protection of control' where each would be guaranteed at least some profit irrespective of efficiency. In 1815, however, the Assize was repealed and

'. . . to those who claimed that removal of control would result in higher bread prices, it was pointed out that in Birmingham, Manchester and Newcastle, where the Assize had been suspended, bread was cheaper than in London'.[3]

The repeal permitted London bakers and those within a 10-mile radius of the City to sell bread at any price provided they made their loaves at standard weights. This last restriction was removed in 1822, and in 1836 bakers throughout the country were freed from price control and allowed to sell loaves of any weight provided it was clearly stated.

'Unfortunately these laws were . . . ambiguous in their wording . . . and magistrates persisted in assuming that any large loaf must weigh two or four pounds precisely.'[4]

[1] Cited *ibid.,* p. 53.   [3] *Ibid.*
[2] Shepphard & Newton, p. 56.   [4] *Ibid.*

As the years passed, bakers were prosecuted for not selling loaves of these weights and generally failed to proffer any adequate defence. This erroneous interpretation of the law became the accepted, *de facto*, regulation governing the marketing of bread.

The National Association of Master Bakers (NAMB),[1] inaugurated in Birmingham in 1887, attempted to put an end to this unsatisfactory state of affairs. It successfully lobbied the Home Secretary, Sir Michael Hicks-Beach, and a clause was inserted into the 1888 Weights and Measures Act designed to free bakers from the risk of prosecution so long as bread was sold by weight and the baker made his customers aware of the weight. Again, however, the clause had been inadequately drafted and a successful prosecution was made under the 1836 Act, which on appeal the High Court upheld as a valid judgement.

There was consternation in the NAMB but no unanimity among its leaders. Some wished for total repeal of the old Bread Laws, others were content with the *de facto*, and now apparently *de jure*, situation. A straight 'Yes : No' referendum was held of all Master Bakers in the United Kingdom. Twenty thousand ballot papers posed the question 'Are you in favour of total repeal of the Bread Laws?'. The result was a shattering indictment of the competitive spirit in the trade and signified an apathetic willingness to hide behind controls. A mere 189 members voted for repeal, 220 voted against.

It is against this background that today's 'standard' loaf must be seen. In many parts of Britain, housewives still refer to the standard loaf as a 'half-loaf'. The standard loaf is directly descended from the 2-lb loaf which has its origins in the accumulated legislation of seven centuries. The 4-lb loaf, London prices for which can be traced at least as far back as 1600 (Chart 1), is now seldom sold. In May 1946, it was reduced by government order to 3½ lbs, and the 'half-loaf' or 'standard' loaf to 1¾ lbs.

With such a genealogy it is tempting to inquire whether or not the sales dominance of the standard loaf reflects consumer

---

[1] The Worshipful (London) Company of Bakers had assisted the authorities in administering the Assize. On abolition in 1815 the Company lost all its main functions and, like most City livery companies and guilds, began to drift further and further away from the trade with which it was originally associated. Most members soon had little, if any, connection with baking.

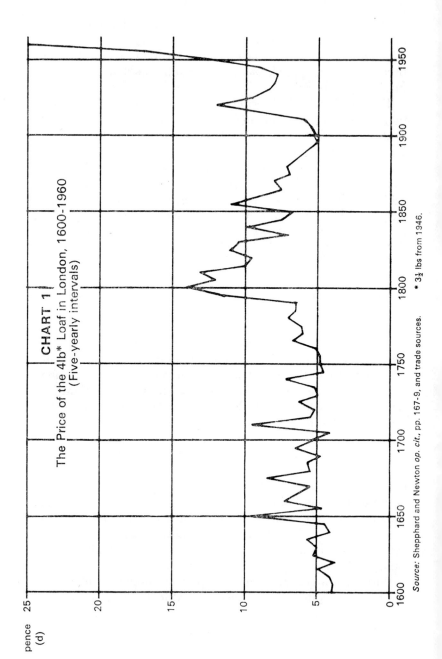

CHART 1

The Price of the 4lb* Loaf in London, 1600-1960
(Five-yearly intervals)

pence (d)

25

20

15

10

5

0

1600 1650 1700 1750 1800 1850 1900 1950

Source: Shepphard and Newton op. cit., pp. 167-9, and trade sources.   * 3½ lbs from 1946.

preferences. Might it not be claimed with equal, or even more, justification that it is a consequence of producer inertia, stimulated by and reinforced with the governmental controls of seven hundred years?

III. COMPETITION REPRESSED?

Competition is the process which begins when consumers attempt to allocate their income between alternative goods or services in the most satisfactory manner. It results in producers striving to manufacture existing products at a lower cost or attempting to produce more attractive products to claim the consumer's attention. The struggle to innovate or to emulate more effectively is of the essence.

Competition has four facets: product, place, price, and promotional rivalry. Profits, other than monopoly profit, are the motivation for and reward gained by producers who satisfy consumer wants.

(i) *Product competition*

The stimulus to rivalry provided by profit can be missing for two main reasons. Legislative controls on prices and profits may remove the incentive to compete, either by curbing monetary rewards or by guaranteeing incomes irrespective of the ability to provide consumer satisfaction. Alternatively, firms may operate in a cartel-like or oligopolistic environment where they tacitly agree to refrain from rivalry, either because fear of being the loser outweighs each firm's wish to gain or because firms are content with the monopoly returns they can extract from the market by acting collusively. The former grouping is the only one of the two which can stifle competition indefinitely. The latter is dependent on some form of gentleman's agreement between firms. But, as Professor George Stigler pithily noted, 'the participants seldom are, or long do'.[1] Profit attracts competition like honey attracts bees. If there are no legal impediments to stop new competitors from entering a market or to restrain firms from behaving in novel ways, competition will drive down selling prices and/or provide more attractive products which will raise buying prices.[2]

[1] G. J. Stigler, *The Theory of Price*, 3rd edition, Macmillan, 1966, p. 230.

[2] To the economist 'price' is not cash price. It is the amount a buyer (seller) is willing to give up (accept) for one more (less) unit of the good in question.

Dominance of the standard loaf

On a narrow definition, competition by product in the bread industry is derisory. Over 70 per cent by weight of all bread sold is categorised as the standard loaf, and a further 11 per cent is merely a small-sized variant (Table VIII). Fancy loaves such as the bloomer, the farmhouse, the buster, the notched cottage and so on form part of the small but recently rising 'other' category in Table VIII, along with rolls, flat breads and proprietary brands such as 'Allinson', 'Hovis', 'Bermaline', 'Procea' and 'Nutrex'.[1]

A possible explanation for the preponderance of the standard loaf is that a standardised shape is required by slicing and wrapping machinery. A second reason is that it is a consequence of oligopolistic inter-dependence. Product similarity facilitates collusive price co-ordination. It is easy for a cartel to identify a seller whose price is out of line if products are standardised and prices are public. Third, to cite a specific reference to bread by the Monopolies Commission: '. . . it may result from the basic nature of the product . . . or . . . from the exhaustion of possibilities for further major product innovation'.[2] Fourth, the dominance of the standard loaf may simply reflect consumer preferences.

Few of these explanations withstand close inspection. Slicing and wrapping machinery can be and is designed to cope with bread of sizes and shapes differing from the 1¾-lb loaf. Far more complex machinery is used in other industries with mass production, where competitors are few, but where product differences are important (cars, chocolate biscuits).

To argue that standardisation is the result of a desire for collusion is difficult. Product uniformity came into being to facilitate control of the trade by government. No baker in this country can recall a time when this was not so. Moreover, the firms have, since the decontrol of bread in 1956, attempted to differentiate their standard product by colour and texture of wrapping (wax paper, clear foil, etc.) and technique of wrapping (e.g. twist and polythene bags). These product variations, and the associated advertising and branding which goes with them, are not the actions to be expected of members of a market-

---

[1] Proprietary breads are named loaves made by either master or plant bakers who produce them from special flours supplied by the manufacturers, who also supply shaped baking tins which emboss the proprietary name on the loaf.

[2] Monopolies Commission, *Parallel Pricing*, Cmnd. 5330, HMSO, 1973, para. 21.

sharing cartel who are indifferent to consumer preferences. Rather they should be seen as competitive behaviour in an industry where intrinsic product variation is difficult because of a real or imagined legal framework, or because of the limitations of plant constructed with that framework in mind.

The Monopolies Commission's view that standardisation is due to the product being 'basic' or technically mature sits uneasily alongside the range of sizes and kinds of breads mentioned earlier. It is not substantiated in its Report[1] and, moreover, contradicts the stance taken by the National Board for Prices and Incomes, which in September 1965 argued strongly for still further standardisation:

> 'Existing equipment would also be used more efficiently if there were longer production runs on fewer types of bread. We have been told of one group producing 75 different types of bread. . . . within the competitive framework as it now is, it is for each company to judge the extent to which it is able to reduce the number of types produced. For the companies to step outside the existing competitive framework and try to reach agreement on the standardisation of types and shapes would raise the question [of] . . . breach of the legislation governing restrictive trade practices. The possible hindrance [this] . . . legislation may place in the way of standardisation . . . we consider would merit the attention of the Government.'[2]

The NBPI apparently wished to strengthen government-backed dampening of industry rivalry even at the expense of existing general industry legislation such as the Fair Trading Act, 1973 (and its earlier antecedents in restrictive trade practices laws) which aim to:

> '[promote] *through competition*, the *reduction of costs* and the *development* and use of new techniques and *new products*, and . . . facilitating the entry of *new competitors into existing markets*'.[3] (My italics.)

A few months later (June 1966) in its next report, the NBPI appeared to change its position. It noted that most bread was in any event standardised, and that non-standard bread, provided it met a consumer want at a price the consumer would willingly pay, was not to be condemned:

[1] Cmnd. 5330.

[2] Cmnd. 2760, para. 39.

[3] *Fair Trading Act*, 1973 (but see above, p. 14, footnote 3).

'. . . 79 per cent of the bread produced . . . by plant bakeries is in the form of standard bread. On average each plant produces about 15 varieties of bread, in the sense of tin weight or flour changes or changes of shapes for bread not in tins. There are nevertheless very wide variations from plant to plant . . . of . . . 379 plants . . . 29 produced over 30 varieties and 60 less than five. . . . *There is evidence that hourly output falls off somewhat as the number of varieties is increased. This does not affect bakery turnover since [they] are able to charge a premium for non-standard bread.*'[1] (My italics.)

By 1970, however, the NBPI had again returned to the theme of increased standardisation, and seemed once more to regard increases in 'hourly output' as more important than meeting consumer demand as reflected by willingness to pay:

'We have examined whether there is scope . . . for measures to contain costs . . . and which, if taken, would contribute to the holding down of prices . . . the retail value of production per man-hour varies substantially. . . . The more productive bakeries are those which have the least number of tin changes per shift and which concentrate on standard loaves.'[2]

The NBPI's desire to see further standardisation was, of course, in the long tradition of government control and regulation of the industry. A homogeneous industry is easier to control than an industry which produces a range of products to meet diverse consumer demands.

It may seem arrogant to dismiss the final explanation: that the dominance of the standard loaf reflects consumer preferences. No doubt many find it the most satisfactory possible product. But with over 700 years of legislation and government exhortation encouraging the industry to move towards standardisation, with government bodies whose priorities are explicitly the 'containment of costs' and 'productivity' based on 'the least number of tin changes', while consumers nevertheless continue to purchase some 20 per cent of all bread in non-standard form, and willingly pay producers a higher price to encourage them to bake such products, the onus of proof is on those who

[1] National Board for Prices and Incomes, *Wages in the Bakery Industry*, Report No. 17, Cmnd. 3019, 1966, Appendix B, paras. 12 and 13.

[2] National Board for Prices and Incomes, *Bread Prices and Pay in the Baking Industry, Second Report*, Report No. 151, Cmnd. 4428, 1970, paras. 64-5. The members were: Rt. Hon. Aubrey Jones, Lord Peddie, Ralph Turvey, Sir Desmond Dreyer, J. E. Mortimer, Professor W. B. Reddaway, Professor H. A. Turner, Professor Joan Woodward, Lord Wright, G. F. Young.

claim that current consumption patterns have not been distorted by centuries of government anxiety to regulate the industry.

(ii) *Place competition*

Place is virtually the only aspect of competition left largely untouched by government control.[1] The forward and backward integration resulted in bread being made available in tens of thousands of non-traditional outlets. The NBPI recorded in 1970 that 130,000 retail outlets sold bread and that 60 per cent of bread sales were made through grocers and supermarkets.[2]

This increase in the availability of bread was viewed with scepticism by some observers. Professor P. E. Hart, Mr M. A. Utton and Mr G. Walshe saw it as the outcome of bilateral monopoly bargaining where the parties eventually agreed to exploit the consumer, maximise joint profits and desist from exploiting each other.

> 'The struggle between the millers and ABF was evidently about the *share* of a joint profit which they could lay claim to. The millers' object was to defend their high returns to capital employed and ABF's object was to appropriate part of these returns.'[3]

This interpretation could be correct in the short run in a true bilateral monopoly. It is more doubtful in the longer run when entry is free, when the bilateral colluders number more than two,[4] and when no government stamp of approval is given to the agreement. The evidence supports the sceptic. Instead of numerous local markets served by small plant or master bakers, often with tied outlets, there is now national competition for shelf space in both bakery and grocery outlets. In the inter-war

---

[1] Even in this element of competition instances of government intervention to protect existing firms can be found. John Stow, referring to the Bread Street Market in London, recorded in the 14th century that bread brought into the City had to be 'two ounces in the penny wheat loaf heavier than the penny wheat loaf baked in the City'. (Shepphard and Newton, *op. cit.*, p. 37.) This ruling was enforced by the Bakers' Company as it assisted the authorities in administering the Assize.

[2] Cmnd. 4428, para. 10.

[3] Hart, Utton and Walshe, *op. cit.*, p. 50.

[4] I have argued elsewhere that even two is too large a number for a prolonged joint profit-maximising bilateral monopoly to persist. Only by integrating vertically into a *single* monopoly unit can the two firms maximise monopoly profits at the expense of the consumer. (*Managerial Economics*, Philip Allen, 1976, pp. 290-6.)

years the consumer benefited from lower prices in new outlets (the grocery chain stores) as the large plant bakers attempted to carve a market for themselves.[1]

20th-century controls initiated: back to the Assize laws?

It is noteworthy that in the inter-war years, when place competition was first beginning to have an impact on the trade, the government introduced the first peace-time monitoring of bread prices in the 20th century. All controls imposed during the First World War were abandoned in 1920 except that which stipulated that bread must be sold in loaves weighing a pound or multiples thereof. (This control was later embodied in the 1926 Weights and Measures Act, thus finally formalising the standards inferred from the 1836 Bread Laws.) A Food Council was established in 1925 with no statutory powers. Its duties were to recommend and publicise bread prices for the London area. The prices recommended were linked to the price of flour, and bread prices elsewhere in Britain were generally linked to London prices. The Council operated until the 1939 war. The duties of the Council, laid down by the 1924 Royal Commission on Food Prices, were:

- to investigate in consultation with local bakers' associations the apparent overlapping, with waste of energy and expenditure in the trade;
- to consider whether consumers who had their bread delivered should not pay for that service so that bread sold over the counter might be cheaper; and
- to maintain close and continuing supervision over price-fixing by bakers' associations and intervene when prices tended to become 'unreasonable'.[2]

In effect the situation was not dissimilar to that of the medieval Assize system of the 13th-18th centuries, which the Bakers' Company helped administer. Local Master Bakers' Associations attempted to fix retail bread prices linked in some way to the 20th-century Food Council's recommendations. The retail Co-operative movement took no active part in the master bakers' agreements but generally followed their lead. The Food Council's recommendations (which presumably it hoped would be maximum prices) became effectively minimum

[1] Above, p. 18 and Table II.

[2] Cited from Shepphard and Newton, *op. cit.*, pp. 172-3.

prices which the trade associations first lobbied for and then attempted to sustain. The objective of the master bakers was to prevent undercutting by non-conforming bakers, or by non-baking retailers or plant bakers. To enforce their agreements, the master baker's associations would threaten to withdraw their members' custom from millers who sold to plant or master bakers who breached the agreed price pattern.[1]

The existence of master bakers' cartels and the effective seal of approval given them by the Food Council was not sufficient to prevent competition by place from benefiting the consumer. Price wars broke out where the master bakers' associations were weak and various outlet types such as plant bakers and grocery chains were relatively strong. Wide regional disparities in price appeared (e.g. in 1925 a 4-lb loaf was obtainable in different areas at prices ranging from $7\frac{1}{2}$d to 11d).[2] And, again, where the master bakers' agreements were successful, support was provided for the view that where regulations allegedly act in the interests of the public they often exist only because a group of sellers have been successful in convincing government officials that what is in the sellers' interests is in the public interest.

Effective competition was consequently not as universal between the wars as it might have been. Restrictive trade practices reinforced by regulatory behaviour stunted its growth. It was not until the Resale Prices Act of 1964 (which abolished resale price maintenance) and the invocation of the 1956 Restrictive Trade Practices Act against the industry (in 1957) that place competition[3] began again to have a significant meaning for the consumer.

(iii) *Price competition*
The suppression of price competition made possible by the Assize laws in collusion with the Bakers' Company ceased when the laws were repealed and bakers outside London, unaffected by the Assize, behaved competitively. Similarly, the price-fixing behaviour of master bakers (with the tacit approval of the Food Council) became less than effective when the plant

[1] *Departmental Committee on Distribution and Prices of Agricultural Produce,* Interim Report No. 4, 1924, para. 162.

[2] Maunder, *op. cit.,* p. 50.

[3] In the sense that different types of retail outlet (e.g. supermarkets) could offer the same product at different prices.

bakers and multiple retailers refused to abide by the agreed prices. A competition-suppressing axis of government and industry was formed again, however, in 1941 when the Federation of Wholesale and Multiple Bakers (FWMB) was founded.

War-time subsidy and price control

The FWMB was given the role of assisting the Ministry of Food in implementing the bread subsidy and price control schemes, which were to continue to 1956. On the outbreak of war in 1939 the government placed controls on the extraction rate[1] of flour and on its price. Bread was controlled by the Bread (Control and Maximum Prices) Order of 1941. The price of bread was fixed at 2d per lb in England and Wales, a figure slightly lower than previous Food Council recommendations, since the Ministry contended that costs would fall with a reduction in the range of permissible breads.

The bread subsidy began in December 1940—a straight 4s. per sack (280 lbs) of flour rebate paid directly to bakers. Ultimately the subsidy was payable only on the 'National' loaf, introduced in March 1942, when the extraction rate of flour milling was raised from 73 to 85 per cent and true white bread ceased. The subsidy was designed to give the industry an average profit of 5s. per sack while holding the price of the National loaf steady. The system operated against the interests of the master bakers. By 1952 the average net profit of plant bakers per sack had reached 6s. $0\frac{1}{2}$d, and the equivalent for master bakers was 2s. $10\frac{1}{2}$d.[2] Without the subsidy master bakers, with higher unit costs than plant bakers, would have been making a loss on bread production. Moreover, master bakers who could have had low unit costs were unable to compete by reducing price to expand throughput to achieve such costs; and equally they were unable to compete by product by making the varieties of bread that might have commanded a higher price and so increased profit per sack.

[1] Wholemeal (or wholewheat) flour includes the whole of the wheatgrain. Nothing is taken away from or added to the milled wheat. Wheatmeal flour is a brown flour from which the coarsest branny particles have been removed. It contains 80-90 per cent of the original wheat. All of the branny skin and that part of the grain from which the embryo wheat plant grows, the wheatgerm, is removed in the milling of white flour. It contains only 70-72 per cent of the original weight of wheat. These percentages are the 'extraction rates'.

[2] *Hansard*, 30 May, 1952, col. 1854. The FWMB undertook sample costings which were supplied to the Ministry.

For a number of years the smaller bakers lobbied the government for a variable subsidy to offset their increased cost disadvantage from the flat-rate subsidy. For a brief period before 1945 they succeeded. But it was not until 1953 that they achieved their aim more permanently. An additional subsidy for all bakers was introduced of 4s. per sack on the first 25 sacks of weekly output; clearly it was of more value to the small producer than to the plant baker with a throughput of several hundred sacks per week.

This action, taken explicitly to neutralise the favourable effects which the previous subsidy structure had had on the plant baker, was too little and too late. More and more master bakers stopped baking the National loaf and either went out of business or retailed bread bought from a plant. The number of bakers claiming the subsidy in the UK dwindled steadily from 1942 to 1955:

(to nearest hundred)

1942	20,600	1951	14,900
1945	18,200	1954	13,800
1948	16,900	1955	12,500

When decontrol began to be a foreseeable reality in the mid-1950s, bakers who had benefited most were (predictably) the opponents. They

'were to be found mainly among the big bakers. . . . The freedom group consisted mainly of those enterprising bakers and individualistic bakers who were anxious to make better bread and charge accordingly for it'.[1]

Moreover, as Table VI indicates, the rate of decline in bread consumption did not accelerate after the subsidy was removed. Probably this was partly due to advertising which offset the higher price, and partly to improvement in quality.

The quality of the product had, indeed, improved despite the subsidy—linked to the National loaf which was made from flour of an 85 per cent extraction rate. The wartime control limiting the extraction rate to 85 per cent was relaxed by the Flour Order, 1953, which permitted any extraction rate provided only that flours of below an 80 per cent rate were enriched with specified nutrients to replace those lost in the removal of the bran and the wheatgerm. When bread became

---

[1] Shepphard and Newton, *op. cit.*, pp. 177-8.

available from the two flours the products were virtually indistinguishable; as a consequence the higher-priced, unsubsidised non-National loaf did not sell. (In 1953 it achieved a market share of 4·4 per cent, which fell to 2·4 per cent by the end of 1953, and by 1955 had dropped to 0·8 per cent.)[1] The Report of the Panel on the Composition and Nutritive Value of Flour said:

> '. . . competition to meet the demands of bakers for white flours has been so keen that, without an effective means of enforcement, it has been impossible to prevent a progressive lowering of the extraction rate of national flour. . . . The Panel is impressed by the demand for white flour and white bread. The professional pride of the miller in producing as clean and white a flour as possible is one reason for this preference . . . a further influence is the preference of the bakers . . . they find it easier to handle and from [it] they can produce more appetising bread. . . . finally the public prefer bread . . . made with the white kinds of flour. The Panel believes that [these] pressure[s] . . . led to the acknowledged infringement of the Flour Order, 1953'.[2]

So, in the long run, competitive forces ensured that the public obtained the bread it preferred (and thus avoided the 'grey' National loaf). Nevertheless, in the interim, the number of competitors in the industry had been reduced, exit from the industry had increased, and the competitive outcome may well have been less favourable than it would have been had the regulations been absent.

Industry reaction to price decontrol (1956)

Although price competition was again legally permitted after 1956, the FWMB had, for the whole of its existence, assisted government in fixing prices. This habit, naturally, proved too strong to break instantaneously. Between 1956 and 1959 price-fixing agreements were made between the FWMB, the NAMB and their Scottish counterparts. Members of each of these organisations had apparently benefited from collusive behaviour in the past and presumably hoped to do so in the future. Moreover, was not price control in the interest of the consumer? The Minister of Agriculture, Mr Heathcoat Amory, had gone as far as to request the industry to use their new freedom 'in a statesmanlike manner, having regard to the economic position of the country'.[3]

[1] *Ibid.*, p. 80.   [2] Cited *ibid.*, p. 80.   [3] Maunder, *op. cit.*, p. 52.

Again, not until the industry faced the Restrictive Trade Practices Court did explicit collusion cease, and even then the benefits of price competition did not start to appear until the traditions of government/industry price agreements were broken by the rivalry of *large-scale retailers* in the 1960s.[1]

(iv) *Competition in promotion*

Promotional competition has, like the other forms, been subject to periodic control. In the 17th and 18th centuries this control may have been no bad thing if some reporters are to be believed. 'At times there was bedlam in the streets while voices, horns and bells competed with each other'[2] to sell bread or solicit housewives' dough for baking. As a consequence the Lord Mayor decreed that 'no baker shall . . . blow any horn or ring or sound any bell . . . in the streets'. Below-the-line promotion[3] was common then as now. And servants hired to hawk and deliver bread in the markets were often given thirteen loaves to the dozen as an inducement to increase sales. The bakers' dozen was the precursor of the deliveryman's commission of the 1970s.[4]

Bread advertising was banned during World II and the ban continued until the removal of the bread subsidy in 1956. In keeping with the government-sponsored cartel-like atmosphere which pervaded the industry through to 1956 and beyond, one of the first major bread advertisers was the Flour Advisory Bureau. The FAB is the public relations arm of the National Association of British and Northern Irish millers. It advertised heavily in the mass media in the 1950s with the object of promoting bread as a generic commodity rather than as a branded good. As the competitive atmosphere in the

---

[1] The 1977 Monopolies and Mergers Commission Report states that from the end of 1959 until 1965 firms 'discussed with the Ministry and *agreements were reached* (my italics) as to the timing and, presumably, the amount of [price] increases'. (HC 412, para. 213.) That is, government/bread industry collusion continued from the time price-fixing agreements were outlawed until the year in which price controls were reimposed.

[2] Shepphard and Newton, *op. cit.*, p. 32.

[3] 'Below-the-line' expenditures are all costs (exclusive of normal media advertising) incurred by firms with the deliberate intention of promoting sales of their product. Thus in-store displays, coupon offers or competitions which require production of the product's wrapper as a condition of entry are all examples of 'below-the-line' promotions.

[4] In addition to their basic wage the earnings of bread lorry drivers are linked to the volume of bread they deliver or sell to their wholesale buyers.

CONSEQUENCES—

The importance of the argument for the reader

1 CONSUMERS would have wider variety in the price and in the range of bread. Their choice would be increased.

2 THE BIG THREE baking firms would not require to cross-subsidise their baking from their milling activities. They would be able to concentrate on the stage (or stages) of the productive process in which they were most efficient and hence most profitable. Firms would be structured according to what the consumer in the *market* required, and not by extraneous and irrelevant influences of self-interested politicians in *government*.

3 INDEPENDENT PLANT BAKERS would be able to enter into trading relationships with their customers unfettered by negotiations or agreements between the Big Three and the government.

4 SMALL MASTER BAKERS would continue in competition with bigger bakers by offering consumers differing combinations of price and product quality. Their success in competing with the big bakers would then be decided by *themselves* and their *customers,* and not helped or hindered by government subsidy to, or price control of, the plant bakers.

5 RETAILERS, like bakers, would be able to offer the consumer the type of bread she wants at the price she is willing to pay. Since consumers have diverse wants, a diversity of retail choice would persist and more accurately reflect consumer wants than would a retail structure determined by government or trade union restrictions on trade between baker, retailer and housewife.

6 EMPLOYEES in bread delivery would, by serving consumer wants as reflected by retailer purchases, serve their self-interest more effectively. Deliverymen would obtain both increased security of employment and higher earnings.

7 POLITICIANS would retain the power to aid the poor in buying bread, to promote competition within the industry, to control the economy in general, but their attempts to manage the minutiae of the industry, not very successful in the past, would end.

8 BUREAUCRATS would lose power in advising on the pricing, output, quality, promotion and other decisions made by firms, which has led to a higher priced, more uniform product and a dampening of competition.

9 TAXPAYERS would see politicians and bureaucrats removed from a function they do not have to perform —the setting of the price and other conditions of sale of a normal commercial product—and freed for services that only government can perform.

10 STUDENTS AND TEACHERS OF ECONOMICS would receive empirical reinforcement of the view that textbooks have generally neglected non-price competition, and that all forms of competition are important in maximising consumer satisfaction.

11 THE OFFICE OF FAIR TRADING AND THE MONOPOLIES COMMISSION would be instructed to examine and appraise all impediments to competition, whether from activities of firms, trade unions or government legislation.

12 TRADE UNIONS, like firms, would be subject to the provisions of the government's competition policy. Suppliers of labour would no more be allowed to exert monopoly power against the interest of the consumer than suppliers of goods or other services.

industry changed, however, the relative weight of FAB advertising came to be dwarfed by branded bread advertising. In the 1950s the FAB's advertising budget ran at approximately £500,000 per annum, in the 1960s it fell, and although it rose on occasion in the 1970s to £500,000 again, in real terms it was worth considerably less than it had been, and amounted to only about 20 per cent of all advertising expenditure on bread.

IV. COMPETITION—ADVANCE AND RETREAT

Cartel-like behaviour usually cannot long survive without the buttress of government support. The removal of the bread subsidy and of price control in 1956 and the judgement of the Restrictive Practices Court against the industry in 1959 encouraged the re-emergence of competition.

(i) *Prohibition of price fixing*

The Federation of Wholesale and Multiple Bakers began to recommend minimum selling prices to its members in September 1956. The practice was referred to the Court in July 1957, and in April 1958 the Federation changed its behaviour, presumably to strengthen its defence before the Court. The recommendations became maximum, not minimum, selling prices, and were based on cost surveys of member firms, a practice pursued until 1956 but abandoned. In addition, the industry recommended a standard discount structure for wholesale buyers (a flat 12½ per cent on retail price irrespective of retail-customer size or location).

The Federation defended itself under gateway 'b' of the Restrictive Trade Practices Act: that the 'removal of the restriction would deny other specific and substantial benefits to the public'. Among the arguments put to justify it were:

   (i) a predictable rate of output was required to encourage investment in capital equipment;

  (ii) recommended maximum prices prevented adherents to the agreement from charging more;

 (iii) price was not an important competitive weapon since geographical expansion would not be practicable due to the difficulty of providing fresh bread distant from source of production;

(iv) the recommended prices were not too high since the Federation had to take account of the possibility that multiple retailers would begin baking if they judged their suppliers were acting monopolistically;

(v) the Federation was sensitive to public opinion;

(vi) a price war would drive more independent bakers out of business and deprive rural customers of supply.

The Court ruled against the industry and held that the costing formula used in setting prices was inadequate to protect the consumer. It was based on outdated wartime conditions. Moreover, when the Federation changed from minimum to maximum price recommendations in 1958 there was no alteration in the recommended prices. The maximum was a *de facto* minimum. Also, given decline in total demand, if a firm wished to maintain production as stated by the Federation, the consequence should have been a fall in price.

(ii) *Increased consumer choice*

After nearly seven centuries of control the bread industry was free to compete in price, product, place and promotion.[1] From 1956 to 1959 the industry had fought to retain the shadow of protection. The 1959 judgement accelerated the appearance of competition, but the competitive behaviour would still have appeared without it (as with Allied Bakeries' backward integration before and after the war).

Product competition increased, and so accordingly did the range of choice. Allied Bakeries, which produced 30 types of bread in 1957, had widened its range to 52 by 1964.[2] 'Tiger' bread was introduced by ABF in 1967 as a long, relatively narrow 14-oz loaf, the then optimum shape for putting in a twist-and-wrap polythene bag. The attraction of the wrapping material, and its preservation of moisture content and so freshness of the loaf, resulted in the consumer willingly paying a higher price. But the premium ABF obtained from 'Tiger' was short-lived. Other firms were attracted by the additional profits ABF were earning as a reward for innovation, and bagging technology was soon available for the standard 28-oz

---

[1] Save only that breads over a stated weight had to be sold in fractions or multiples of the 1¾-lb standard loaf embodied in the Weights and Measures Acts, and that flour could not fall below a stated extraction rate without an addition of specified nutrients.

[2] *Financial Times*, 14 September, 1964.

[41]

loaf. RHM were the first to introduce a bagged standard loaf ('Mother's Pride'), and they in turn were quickly followed by ABF's 'Sunblest'. 'Tiger' reaped the rewards of the innovator, achieved a not insignificant brand share, but declined to only minor importance when its advantages were more widely available at a lower price.

RHM were also the first to move away from the oblong standard loaf. RHM bakeries were re-equipped with round tins at a cost approaching £1 million,[1] and the resulting cylindrical loaf was christened 'Big T' and sold throughout the country, except in the South-East. The large round slices appealed to many consumers, who willingly paid a price $\frac{1}{2}$p higher than that for the standard loaf. After a number of successful local market tests in 1971, the near-national launch resulted in 'Big T' achieving 15 per cent of total bread sales by 1973.[1] (The South-East market, according to RHM spokesmen, requires a 'more sophisticated' product than the 'masculine' 'Big T'.[1])

Spillers-French, just before it merged with the CWS bread interests, brought out a premium bread to complement its 'Wonderloaf'. It was given the brand-name 'Homepride' and capitalised on the consumer goodwill for the best-selling 'Homepride' household flour. In turn it was joined by 'Homepride Danish King', a 14-oz loaf not dissimilar in size from a standard loaf, which meets a consumer demand for a light bread for toast and sandwiches.

Failure to meet competition: self-bake bread

The competition for consumers was also marked by failure. The bread firms could not make customers buy what they did not want. In the late 1960s and into the 1970s the reaction in the media and elsewhere to the uniform, soft, fresh and very bland standard loaf became ever more strident.[2] To counter it, and meet an apparent consumer demand, the firms produced a range of self-bake bread. In 1970 'Mother's Pride' alone spent £240,000 advertising 'Take and Bake' white bread and a further £50,000 promoting the brown equivalent. (These figures formed 16 per cent of total bread industry advertising

[1] *Daily Mirror*, 8 November, 1973.

[2] *Sunday Times* (16 June, 1974) cynically noted that the 'chemists and manufacturers' are 'known for advertising purposes as bakers'.

expenditure in that year.)[1] 'Take and Bake', 'Sunblest's' 'Heat and Eat' and 'Cottage Kitchen', and Spiller's 'Home Bake', however, never achieved significant sales. After a brief surge of enthusiasm, housewives soon discovered that bakery bread was more satisfactory. The work and cost and time required to heat their domestic ovens to a high temperature plus the two-hour cooling period before the loaf could be sliced and eaten soon disenchanted the consumer. The firms had misjudged the market's demand and paid the penalty of failure.

In the brown bread segment of the market competition was equally intense. RHM's 'Hovis' after several years of brand leadership came under pressure from Allied's 'Vitbe'. In early 1976 'Vitbe' brought out 'Hi Bran', the first nationally-promoted high-fibre brown loaf. By early 1977 'Vitbe' had become the brand leader[2] in the brown bread market and had done so with a smaller advertising budget[3] than 'Hovis' but a wider range of products.

The bread market, then, is no sleepy oligopoly where a few dominant firms can produce a uniform product at a tightly co-ordinated price. It is an industry where competition by innovation is rife. When specific products fail to or cease to provide consumer satisfaction their market share declines. Firms can maintain their market standing only if they con-tinuously provide an array of products with the characteristics consumers want. They cannot reach forward to the consumer and, as Professor J. K. Galbraith has frequently said, by heavy advertising persuade or manipulate the market to buy what consumers do not want.[4]

It is possible that in the short run markets may work in ways which do not benefit the consumer. In the long run this cannot happen without government support. In the short run it can occur if firms can successfully collaborate, even if only

[1] Data abstracted from *MEAL, Monthly Digest of Advertising Statistics,* December 1970.

[2] Trade sources.

[3] In the first nine months of 1976 'Hovis's' budget was £631,500 and 'Vitbe's' £363,000 (*MEAL* data).

[4] *The Affluent Society*, Hamish Hamilton, 1958 (Pelican, 1962), Chapter 11; *The New Industrial State*, Hamish Hamilton, 1967 (Penguin, 1969); *Economics and the Public Purpose*, Andre Deutsch, 1974 (Penguin, 1975); *The Age of Uncertainty*, BBC/Andre Deutsch, 1977, Chapter 9. Critiques of Galbraith's argument will be found in G. C. Allen, *Economic Fact and Fantasy*, Occasional Paper 14, IEA, 2nd Edition, 1969; and Milton Friedman, *From Galbraith to Economic Freedom*, Occasional Paper 49, IEA, 1977.

temporarily, or if the countervailing power of intermediaries in the market-place is used to the detriment of the consumer. As will be described later, in the bread market this bargaining power has conferred benefits and imposed costs on the consumer.

(iii) *The consumer or the retailer?*

In its defence before the Restrictive Practices Court the FWMB argued that the standard fixed 12½ per cent discount to retailers was desirable to prevent an upward drift of retail prices. The Council for the Registrar of Restrictive Trade Practices cited a letter (in court) written by the Secretary of the FWMB to a regional association whose members had been under pressure to grant higher discounts to a multiple retailer:

> 'It is obvious that wholesale discounts must be kept to a minimum, not only for the protection of retail business, but also in the public interest . . . and [so] prevent the outbreak of price cutting wars which were so ruinous 20 years ago'.[1]

In other words, gross margins were to be guaranteed to all retailers irrespective of their relative bargaining power with the bakers on the one hand, or their efficiency in selling bread to the consumer on the other. The Court ruled against fixed standard discounts and retailers who could began to nudge discounts upwards towards 18-20 per cent.[2]

Retailers were unable to pass on the benefit of their increased discounts to consumers because of resale price maintenance (RPM).[3] Even after the abolition of RPM in 1964, the Prices and Incomes Board, chaired by Mr Aubrey Jones,[4] did not believe advantage was to be gained by the consumer:

> 'In our view there are special factors in the bread industry which militate against price competition . . . demand . . . is inelastic; a reduction in the price does not enlarge the market; *nor does any practicable reduction significantly enlarge the market share of one competitor against another.* . . . In addition, the short shelf life and bulkiness of bread make it *an unsuitable product with which to*

---

[1] Cited in Maunder, *op. cit.*, p. 62.

[2] Spillers was the first baker to crack, awarding Tesco a 15 per cent discount in 1961.

[3] B. S. Yamey, *Resale Price Maintenance and Shoppers' Choice,* Hobart Paper No. 1, IEA, 1960 (4th Edition, 1964), p. 8.

[4] Its other members were Lord Peddie, D. A. C. Dewdney, H. A. M. Marquand, Robert Willis and Dr Joan Mitchell.

stimulate turnover by price cutting; supermarkets in particular are inclined to this view. In such circumstances we feel that the general uniformity of price . . . is probably inherent·in the nature of the industry'.[1]

Most of the assertions in this quotation are nonsensical. For example, (market) price elasticity has very little to do with the individual firm's pricing or output decisions in conditions of competition. This was illustrated a mere 16 months later. Several retail co-operatives in the Manchester area reduced bread prices by 2d (from 1s. 5½d to 1s. 3½d, or 11½ per cent) in January 1967, and in the North East a consortium of retail co-operatives initiated a price cut of 4d. Sales of bread in the latter group rose by 300 per cent and the success of bread as a loss leader was shown by an increase in sales of 27 per cent on other lines sold at normal prices.[2] The precedent set by these co-operatives was soon followed by other retailers such as Tesco, Woolworth and Sainsbury. The advent of competition by price, stimulated by efficient retailers within a permissive framework, was working in the consumer interest. Not that the bakers necessarily approved. Indeed 'the baking firms [did] not support such campaigns and offer[ed] no encouragement . . . one [firm] attempted to induce a retailer to rescind his price reduction in September 1967'.[3]

Countervailing (retailer) power: day-dated bread

Countervailing power can also work against the consumer interest. In May 1969 'Sunblest' launched its 'Happy' loaf. Every (standard) loaf was packaged in the bright colour of the day and had imprinted all over the wrapper 'Happy Monday', or 'Tuesday' . . . until Saturday, with 'Happy Weekend'. At the time of its launch 'Sunblest' was running second to 'Mother's Pride' in market share terms and the 'Happy' loaves pushed it into brand leadership.[4] Exhaustive interviews of housewives all over Britain had preceded the launch.[5] Consumers wanted freshness.

The multiple retailers reacted by pressing for a sale-or-return system with the bakers to avoid obviously day-old bread on their shelves. Previously sale-or-return had been unknown in

[1] Cmnd. 2760, para. 45 (my italics).
[2] *The Grocer*, 4 February, 1967, p. 25.
[3] *The Times*, 26 September, 1967.
[4] Trade sources.
[5] *Financial Times*, 30 May, 1969.

the trade—the retailer either bore the cost of over-ordering by wastage or by reducing his price late in the afternoon, or passed on the product to an unwitting customer. Independent grocers did not have the power to demand a sale-or-return deal but they could withdraw their custom from 'Sunblest'. They did not wish to incur the heavy marginal costs implicit in under- or over-ordering to obtain the small marginal benefits of providing shelf-space for one brand. ABF then began to supply independent retailers with bread in standard 'Sunblest' wrappers. The proportion of retailers so supplied began to rise, as did the volume of returned bread, and by the end of 1971 ABF decided to withdraw the 'Happy' loaf.

The outcome might have been different had there been no multiplicity of middlemen. 'Happy' bread failed because the benefits it provided for the consumer, reflected in a market-share increase for the manufacturer, were less than the costs (of more careful purchasing schedules) incurred in aggregate by all retailers. Care in purchasing, however, entails a fixed, managerial expense which does not vary with turnover. Thus a combined manufacturer/retailer, with fewer outlets but the same volume of sales, would have reaped the same benefits as did the 'Happy' loaf but with substantially lower costs.[1]

This is a situation where economies of marketing external to the individual firm exist.[2] It is not, however, an argument for a monolithic baking/retailing concern. Such a firm would be wholly indifferent to consumer preferences (although in principle it could recoup from the market-place the costs of benefits it had conferred). Rather it is one kind of market imperfection which government legislation could be designed to correct. The current practice of date-coding bread wrappers may be satisfactory to the retailer who knows the code, but is of little use to the consumer.

---

[1] This may be one explanation why Marks and Spencer Ltd find it commercially attractive to identify the relative freshness of their baked goods. They sell only products marked with the 'St. Michael' brand name and no competing brands occupy adjacent shelf-space. The firm incurs all the (fixed) costs involved in careful purchasing/production scheduling, but it and its customers also reap all the resulting benefits. No other brands but 'St Michael' are available on the shelves, and 'St Michael' brands are exclusive to Marks and Spencer.

[2] An 'external economy' (externality) exists when one party benefits another (deliberately or not) and cannot make the recipient of the benefit pay for all the costs he, the creator of the benefit, has incurred.

(iv) *The consumer or the politician?*

Consumers, manufacturers and retailers benefit from the production of bread. Politicians also have a stake in the industry. The price of bread has always been a live *political* issue.

No sooner had bread flung off the last vestiges of control in 1964 when RPM was abandoned than it became subject to investigation in 1965, 1966 and 1970 (twice) by the newly-formed Prices and Incomes Board.[1] The 1965 Report rejected the industry's claim for a 1d per loaf increase and recommended instead a deferred increase six months later. The 1966 Report related primarily to wages, while the first 1970 Report approved a 1d increase in the price of the standard loaf, and the second covered a much wider brief relating to industrial efficiency, prices, costs and labour relations. Competition in list prices consequently did not in effect exist between 1965 and 1970, although, as we have seen, discounts were varied between sellers and buyers of bread, and retail price competition was on occasion intense.

In spite of competition and regulation, bread prices continued to rise. The price controls of the 1964-70 Labour Governments were abandoned by the Conservatives. But, as in the 1959-64 period, bread prices were still not exempt from government oversight. The Conservative Government

'substituted a system of voluntary notification of intended price changes for certain products, including bread. . . . an increase . . . was made under these arrangements in November 1970. . . . From mid-July 1971 . . . bread pricing decisions were influenced by undertakings given by producers to the CBI and by increasing government concern about the amount and timing of food price increases generally'.[2]

In November 1972 a price freeze held the price of bread steady for more than six months.

Political price control and subsidy again: who benefits?

The Price Commission, created by the Counter-Inflation Act of 1973, had the task of administering the Government's Price Code. It has scrutinised applications for bread price increases on a number of occasions. By the time of the February

---

[1] Its Reports were published respectively as Cmnd. 2760, Cmnd. 3019, Cmnd. 4329 and Cmnd. 4428.

[2] HC 412, para. 222.

1974 election campaign Mr Harold Wilson was citing the price of bread as an election issue. On 21 March, 1974, the Government announced it would subsidise bread at a rate of one half-penny per standard loaf. This was increased to 2 pence in May 1974 and reached an eventual peak of 3 pence (Table X), with lower figures for 14-oz loaves. In the fiscal year 1974-75 the bread subsidy cost the government (or rather the taxpayer) £63·4 million.[1]

Who have been the real beneficiaries of government's apparent concern for the consumer? The politician presumably hopes to benefit from voter approval of his activity. It is far from clear that such approval would be justified. Before introducing the bread subsidy the purpose of the Secretary of State for Prices and Consumer Protection seemed directed more towards controlling price than providing consumers with the products they wanted and were prepared to pay for. Mrs Shirley Williams 'asked the industry first to examine the chances of producing a "national loaf", *perhaps of inferior quality*' (my italics).[2] This 'request' hardly smacks of true devotion to the interests of the public.

What were the outcomes? Retailers generally were bound by the Price Code which stipulated that gross percentage margins must be 10 per cent below those of the base reference year (usually an accounting year ending before April 1973). This rule inevitably had the effect that retailers who could, for whatever reason, negotiate larger discounts with the bread firms did so, and either cut prices on bread or on other goods to keep their average margin within the limits of the Price Code. Since bread (and other bakery products) provides high absolute profit per foot of shelf space in the average super-market (bakery goods occupy under 10 per cent of display space and provide over 20 per cent of profit),[3] the natural reaction of the grocery trade was to concentrate its selling efforts on bread, where profits were relatively high, and allow slower-selling, costlier-to-market goods to bring down the average gross margin to within the Price Code limits.

So, while the bakers engaged in price competition with large discounts on list price, the Government provided them with a

[1] *Economic Progress Report,* No. 60, March 1975.

[2] *The Times,* 18 April, 1975.

[3] *Ibid.*

facilitating subsidy which the retailers used to cross-subsidise other activities.

In April 1974 *The Grocer* commented:

'It would be difficult to prove, but there is a feeling that at this moment many multiples have stopped cutting the price of bread as they were or could'.[1]

There was another reason. The retailing industry was anticipating a maximum price order to be placed on bread by the Government. If this expectation was to be justified (as it was), the grocers did not want to have their prices held down from an uncertain base date.[2]

Effects of uncertainty and profit controls

Political uncertainty and blanket profit margin controls thus encouraged retailers to behave as they would have done had they been members of a formal cartel: bread prices were maintained at a high level. Since there were no legal impediments to competition, however, the cartel-like behaviour did not persist. The stimulus of the profit gained by the multiple retailers from the manufacturers in the form of large discounts motivated other groups of retailers to emulate them and to cut their bread prices. In September 1974 several major voluntary chains of independent grocers, which had previously received only the standard $12\frac{1}{2}$ per cent discount from the manufacturers, negotiated additional discounts ranging from $2\frac{1}{2}$ to 10 per cent for their members. The Mace and VG groups concluded deals with RHM, while Spar-Vivo and A & O International negotiated similar trades with Spillers. Most of these deals were accompanied by large advertising campaigns and lower bread prices to the consumer. In most instances the grocers began to deal only with the manufacturing group with which their chain had negotiated the special discounts, thus economising on transport costs by minimising dual deliveries by two or more bread firms to one retailer. In at least one case (A & O-Spillers) the manufacturer provided specialised merchandising services and display stands tailor-made for the small floor space of the typical independent grocer's shop.[3]

These competitive benefits were soon removed. Mrs Shirley Williams produced the long-anticipated maximum bread Price

[1] *The Grocer*, 10 April, 1974, p. 8.

[2] Reported *ibid.*

[3] *The Grocer*, August-October 1974 (various issues).

[49]

Order in early November 1974: it showed the maximum retail prices in five areas of the UK and for eight types of bread.[1]

The prices to be charged by retailers were the lower of those shown in the Order or those on the date (March 1974) when the subsidy was introduced.[2]

So one of the explanations given above (p. 49) for the high bread prices maintained by the multiple grocers in the face of high discounts was substantiated. The other contention made repeatedly in this *Paper*, that only government can persistently maintain a non-competitive situation, also received support. Within a month of the Price Order Mrs Williams announced to the House of Commons that all discounts of over $22\frac{1}{2}$ per cent on retail prices were to be banned, and that any deals concluded since 3 September, 1974, were to be rendered null and void. 'Discounts' were defined very widely to include benefits in cash or kind to retailers, their staff or their head offices. More specifically, items were included as 'discounts' explicitly back-dated to September: financial incentives on non-bread bakery goods and in-store display fixtures. Both had figured prominently in the voluntary chains' deals.

The voluntary chains protested against the ruling, but to no avail. Other spokesmen in the industry suggested it was equitable since the multiples were suffering a discount freeze at best, and a substantial cut in discounts at worst. (Some margins had risen as high as 40 per cent.)

There is thus little evidence from the experience of this industry to support the view that self-interested politicians (who seek to maximise votes) will serve the consumer any better than self-interested business men (who seek to maximise profits). Indeed the reverse appears to be true. Consumers can have more confidence in the workings of ordinary commercial markets, with all their faults, than in the highly uncertain mechanism of the governmental process.[3]

Yet another example of how government thwarted the industry's willingness to compete by price, and so harmed the consumer interest, is the polythene-bagged standard loaf.

---

[1] The 1266 Assize tables related only to London, and applied to only four types of bread (above, p. 25); otherwise it was a case of *plus ça change, plus c'est la même chose.*

[2] *The Bread Prices Order,* 1974, No. 1711; and *The Grocer,* 2 November, 1974.

[3] These and similar issues are further discussed in I. R. C. Hirst, 'Consumer Choice and Collective Choice', in I. R. C. Hirst and W. Duncan Reekie (eds.), *The Consumer Society,* Tavistock, 1977, and Tullock, *op. cit.*

'Mother's Pride' was the first to instal the necessary packaging machinery. Other firms could not compete by product until they had purchased similar equipment. But because of the advertising moratorium[1] and discount freeze neither could they compete by promotion, nor by price cutting. ABF and Spillers unsuccessfully petitioned the Government to allow them to sell their (wax-paper wrapped) loaves at a price less than the 'Mother's Pride' product, but to no avail. The firms may have been hoist by their own petard, but this was of little benefit to the consumer.

(v) *The consumer or the producer?*

The consumer had thus been prevented from benefiting from lower retail prices, first, by the multiples maintaining high gross margins because of (justified) fear of a political Order setting maximum prices, and, second, by the Government freezing discounts and retrospectively forcing firms to raise their prices to earlier, less competitive heights. The Government's rationale for the discount freeze was ostensibly to prevent a state subsidy going to the retailer rather than the consumer.[2] But to the extent that this had occurred it was at least partly due to government activity or inactivity in the first instance. The Price Code artificially encouraged retailers to concentrate on the marketing of bread: a product which under normal trading conditions already provided above-average profits per foot of shelf space. It was the uncertainty surrounding the contents and timing of the Price Order that maintained prices at abnormally high levels.

Government-industry leaders' collusion (continued)

The large manufacturers were apparently 'only too glad to have Mrs Williams in the ring as a referee'.[3] Their enthusiasm had indeed been conveyed officially to the Monopolies and Mergers Commission:

> '. . . both RHM and Spillers emphasised to us in mid-1976 the importance which they attached to the continued statutory control of discounts on bread sales'.[4]

[1] Below, p. 52.

[2] 'To ensure that the benefit of bread subsidy was passed on to the consumer, orders were made . . . under the Prices Act, 1974.' (HC 412, para. 232.) In all, 11 orders were passed between October 1974 and July 1977.

[3] *Financial Times*, 18 November, 1976.

[4] HC 412, para. 301.

The familiar cycle of government collusion with the established industry leaders at the expense of competition and the consumer was thus emerging yet again. From the London Bakers' Company (and the Assize Laws, pp. 27n and 33n) to the NAMB (and the Food Council, pp. 34 and 35), the FWMB (and the Ministry of Food's subsidy and control schemes, pp. 36 and 37), and finally the Big Three (with their 'agreements' with the Ministry of Agriculture from 1959 to 1965, p. 39n; and their 'voluntary notifications' to government from 1970 to 1973, p. 47), the pattern was as before.

It should also be pointed out that the Government, by reducing discounts between the bakers and their customers, had damaged relations between baker and retailer. The retail trade may have felt that their margins had been sacrificed for the sake of maintaining a degree of profitability in the baking industry. Hence, given a lack of trust between the two parties, the bakers may have tried to dissuade the Government from a too sudden opting out of the position it had created. (As one large baker remarked to me: 'If we must choose between continued Government interference or be thrown to the wolves, we would opt for the latter.')

The small independent plant bakers, however, were very unhappy about the discount freeze. The Monopolies Commission reported that some independents

'sought permission to grant discounts in excess of those statutorily prescribed on the ground that they needed to do so in order to counter-balance the greater advertising power of the Big Three Groups. At the suggestion of Government, this led to a voluntary agreement whereby the Big Three undertook to refrain from national advertising of their major brands of 28-oz standard bread for a period'.[1]

The agreement lasted for nearly 18 months from January 1975. The 'public relations' conduct of the episode by Mrs Williams and her civil servants was politically astute. Government subsidies, they said, were not being used on 'wasteful' advertising. The frozen discount was not simply being transferred to other forms of promotion. The large bakers were holding down costs and subsidies would not require to be as high as they might otherwise have had to be.

This gracious withdrawal from the competitive fray by the

[1] HC 412, para. 300.

large bakers was, however, not so simple. Total bread advertising did indeed fall, but not dramatically. In 1973 £2·4 million was spent on press and television advertising, in 1974 £1·9 million, and in 1975 £2·0 million.[1] The advertising budget had merely been redirected to other products such as 'slimming' loaves, proprietary breads, non-standard breads, bakery ranges with the same brand names as the relevant standard loaves, and to the regional standard loaves manufactured by the Big Three. Thus in 1974 'Mother's Pride Baker's Basket' had £200,000 worth of advertising support and 'Big T' (not a nationally distributed loaf) £240,000.[1] Similarly, when ABF opened its new regional bakery in the Balmore district of Glasgow, its loaf was promoted as 'Balmore' bread, not as 'Sunblest'.

In this way the competitive position of the independents was further weakened by the Big Three, just as, in the 1940s and 1950s, the competitive position of the master bakers had been weakened by the plant bakers' ability to produce the 'National' loaf at a lower unit cost. In both instances firms were merely following their competitive judgement, but doing so in a framework of rules laid down by government which ensured that the outcome would be one of reduced, not increased, competition. The master bakers were stopped from producing and selling superior bread at a premium price: and the independent plants were stopped from increasing their discounts to compete with the advertising expertise of the Big Three.

Mechanics of bread subsidy encourage collusion

This politically-stimulated collusive behaviour by the Big Three against the rest of the industry and so the consumer was further encouraged by the mechanics of the subsidy. The manufacturers were at one time obliged to consult with one another about the amount of subsidy they wanted to ask. The Secretary of State agreed she would accept full responsibility if as a result the firms were compromised with the Monopolies and Mergers Commission.[2] This sort of politicised environment could only encourage collusive behaviour. Mrs Williams's

---

[1] *MEAL, Monthly Digest of Advertising Statistics* (various issues).

[2] *The Times*, 18 April, 1975. The size of the subsidy paid after each successful claim for a price increase equalled the rise awarded to the firm which gained least from the Price Commission.

successor, Mr Roy Hattersley, apparently adopted this view. To enable bread prices to be determined by competition rather than by government control of discounts, he brought out an Order which once again (from 4 January, 1977) enabled retailers to negotiate whatever discounts they could with manufacturers.

He did not, however, remove the price ceiling on bread. It could be argued that this omission exemplified supreme hypocrisy by the Government. It had brought about a situation of distrust between the bakers and their major customers, but would not allow consequent escalation of discounts to be recovered through the Price Commission. This had the effect of eliminating the minimal profit safeguards allowed under the Price Code. Bread was consequently treated differently from many other foods subject to price control.

Instead, a new range of statutory prices was announced. Table IX shows this range calculated on an assumed 21p maximum price for a standard loaf. Master bakers did not have to start cutting prices below the 21p level as quickly as did grocers and supermarkets. But a supermarket which negotiated a $22\frac{1}{2}$ per cent discount would have to reduce the price by at least 2 pence. (The higher figures in the Table are purely speculative.)

(vi) *The consumer or the trade unionist?*

One group of people did not view Table IX as mainly conjectural. These were the members of the United Road Transport Union (URTU) who deliver bread for the bakers to the supermarkets and whose earnings are heavily dependent on commission on sales. Higher discounts implicitly mean lower earnings, other things equal. The URTU declared that from 4 January, 1977, they would not deliver to shops selling bread at a price more than 4 pence (or sometimes less) below the permitted maximum. On the first day of the dispute ABF publicly announced that it would negotiate discounts no higher than 26·375 per cent with any customer, thus effectively drawing the real teeth from the dispute, and apparently admitting defeat by (or connivance with the objectives of) the union.

> 'Mr. Hattersley's efforts to reintroduce competition have been defeated by an unadmitted but evident corporatist alliance of the bakers and their men.'[1]

[1] *Economist*, 15 January, 1977.

[54]

TABLE IX

THE RANGE OF MAXIMUM BREAD PRICES, JANUARY 1977

(based on maximum recommended retail price of 21p)

Discount given by Manufacturer %	Maximum Permitted Selling Price	
	Supermarkets and Grocers	Master Bakers
0 – 17½	21	21
17½– 20	20½	21
20 – 22½	20	21
22½– 25	19	21
25 – 27½	18	20
27½– 30	17	19
30 – 32½	16	18
32½– 35	15	17
35 – 37½	14	16
37½– 40	13	15
40 – 42½	12½	14
42½– 45	12	13
45 – 47½	11½	12
47½– 50	11	11
50 – 55	10	10
55 – 60	9	9
60 – 65	8	8
65 – 70	7	7
70 – 75	6	6
75 – 80	5	5
80 – 85	4	4
85 – 90	3	3
90 – 95	2	2
95 –100	1	1

Source: Financial Times, 14 December, 1976.

The situation was stabilised not long after, and few if any retailers gained a discount above the 22½ per cent maximum which existed before the lifting of the statutory ceiling.

The conclusion that the union and the manufacturers were in a 'corporatist alliance' was not wholly inaccurate. The unions did not want discounts to escalate. The manufacturers had similar objectives.[1] But the proximate cause of this community of interest was the continuing government-imposed price ceiling on the retail list price of bread. If that situation had not existed manufacturers competing for business would not for long have forfeited the possibility of increased sales and profits if they could have perceived a way out of an apparent *impasse* where unions dominated pricing strategy. They would have reorganised remuneration terms with the drivers, resolved the industrial relations dispute, and again competed for the customer's purchasing power.

ABF's action in announcing maximum terms to the trade thus reflected both trade union pressure to hold discounts down and the impact of a government-imposed price ceiling. But it was also the competitive initiative to be expected from the industry's acknowledged price leader.[2] It provided a starting point in the industry's relationships with its customers after a lengthy period during which it had been unable to negotiate on price. Discounts began to rise again[3] but seldom (if ever) re-achieved the heights ruling before the discount freeze and the URTU action. In short, a powerful pressure group, URTU, was able to exercise its powers as a monopolistic supplier of labour in order to appropriate for its members benefits which would otherwise have reached the consumer *via* the mechanism of higher discounts to and competition between retailers.

V. THE CASE FOR CONTROL

It would be unreasonable to let the case for control go by default. There may be a number of reasons why government should control the bread industry. The arguments which can be advanced are not powerful, and may be invalid.

[1] It has been noted that both RHM and Spillers informed the Monopolies Commission that they opposed removal of the discount freeze. (Above, p. 51.)

[2] Professor George J. Stigler writes that a price leader is the firm whose price adjusts promptly 'to important changes in cost or demand conditions'. Other firms follow in a competitive fashion 'only because, and to the extent that, his price reflects market conditions.' (*The Organisation of Industry*, Richard D. Irwin, 1968, p. 228.)

[3] As time passed competitive forces pushed discounts up towards the 26·375 per cent plus, in some cases, additional assistance for promotions, whilst most minor retailers, who during the discount freeze were pegged to $12\frac{1}{2}$ per cent or 15 per cent discounts, began to receive amounts considerably in excess of these figures, rising, in some cases, to over 26 per cent.

(i) *Maintenance of a low price*

Tables X and XI show that during the decade of least control of the bread market, 1956 to 1965, the recommended selling price of bread rose from an index value of 85·2 (1962 = 100) to 114·8. This was not dissimilar to the rise in the Retail Price Index or in its food component. From 1965 to 1970 the list price was subject to considerable price-cutting by retailers. From 1972 to 1976, the period of tightest control during the span of the tables, the bread price index rose by 169 points, the RPI by 185·5 points and the all-food index by 135·4 points. Even if the list price index does not truly reflect the market price of bread, correction back to 'market' prices by subtracting

TABLE X

THE LIST PRICE OF THE WRAPPED AND SLICED STANDARD LOAF, 1956-77

		Price			Index
		s. d.	pence		(1962=100)
September	1956	11½			85·2
February	1962	1 1½			100
January	1967	1 5½			129·6
February	1971		9½		168·9
February	1974		14½		257·7
				Subsidy	
March	1974		14½*	½p	257·7
May	1974		14½*	2p	257·7
August	1974		14½*	2½p	257·7
January	1975		14½*	3p	257·7
February	1975		16*	2½p	284·4
May	1975		16½*	2½p	293·3
October	1975		16*	2½p	284·4
December	1975		17*	2p	302·2
April	1976		18*	2p	320·0
August	1976		19*	1½p	337·7
October	1976		20*	1½p	355·5
January	1977		21*	1p	373·3
March	1977		22*	1p	391·1
July	1977		23½	nil	417·8

* Includes subsidy.

Source: Federation of Bakers. (Index constructed by the author.)

[57]

TABLE XI

RETAIL PRICE INDEX—MONTHLY AVERAGES,
1956-76

(*16.1.62 = 100*)

	All Items	Food
1956	85·6	90·2
1959	92·0	95·7
1962	101·6	102·3
1965	112·1	111·6
1968	125·0	123·2
1971	153·4	155·6
1974	208·2	230·0
1975*	304·0	331·2
1976*	349·8	404·8

Sources: Annual Abstracts of Statistics.

*Department of Employment Gazettes (year-end figures).

discounts and adding back subsidies would make little differ-ence to the general picture.

Controls have *not* held prices down.

(ii) '*Social*' considerations

A subsidy is a welfare instrument designed to change consumer behaviour at the point of purchase. The general feeling of economic retrenchment in the early 1970s coupled with the bread subsidy and the publicity which surrounded it seem to have accomplished this aim. The steady fall in the consumption of bread was reversed in 1974 for the first time in over 20 years (Table VI). This downward movement enabled the Labour Party to fulfil its election manifesto pledge of February of that year that they would introduce 'a system of food subsidies to help families against increases in [the prices of] essential foods'.

But in Table VII it was noted that bread is no longer an important item of expenditure in either rich or poor households. Even in the poorest households, with weekly income of head of household under £19·50 per week (in 1973), the average weekly consumption of bread per head was less than 1½ standard loaves, or 16 pence in expenditure. Yet in fiscal year 1974-75 the Government subsidised bread to the extent of £63·4 million, a not inconsiderable sum. This figure was dis-tributed fairly evenly over rich and poor alike. (Table VII shows that the two poorest social groupings consumed only 10 and 16 per cent more bread than the average.) So, while the subsidy helped fulfil the electoral pledge of the politicians, it is difficult to see why the poverty-stricken consumer of bread should unknowingly forego a social welfare payment made willingly by government to the wealthy buyer of bread who consumes it mainly as an accompaniment to *pâté de foie gras*. The late Professor R. M. Titmuss argued[1] that the only justification for a 'non-discriminating universalist service' (such as a bread subsidy) was if the cause of the problem could not be identified and offset in some other way. Yet poverty and the inability to pay for the necessaries of life is an identifiable condition. The political kudos and electoral bonus to be gained from the subsidy seem to have carried more weight than Titmuss's warning that 'Universalism is not, by itself alone, enough . . . This much we have learnt . . .'. Those who lost from the political decision to provide a universal subsidy were those most in need of help.

(iii) *Abuse of monopoly power*

This *Paper* contains numerous examples of market exploitation by firms or groups of firms with some degree of market power. On occasion millers, sometimes bakers, and at other times retailers have failed to act in a truly competitive manner.[2] A widely acknowledged function of government is to promote industrial efficiency and consumer protection through competition. Yet virtually every example of such non-competitive behaviour has been condoned by, encouraged by, or resulted from government activity.

Bread baking has been scrutinised under government competition policy on three occasions: in 1958 under the Restrictive Trade Practices Act; in 1973 when it was one of five industries examined in the Monopolies Commission Report on *Parallel Pricing*;[3] and, most recently, in the Monopolies Commission Report of 1977.[4]

The Big Three are not 'monopolists' in legal terms. None of

---

[1] *Commitment to Welfare*, Allen and Unwin, 1968, pp. 34-5.

[2] A trade union, URTU, has also acted monopolistically (above, pp. 54-56).

[3] Cmnd. 5330.

[4] HC 412.

them supplies 25 per cent or more[1] of the bread market; and, although in aggregate they supply more than that proportion, their uniformity of list prices was not found by the Monopolies Commission to represent a 'significant restriction of competition'.[2] Neither are they 'monopolists' in the economic meaning of the word. Strictly, monopoly ('single seller') exists when a firm or a group of firms supplies the total market for a product; none of the Big Three falls within this definition.

Nevertheless, they may possess a degree of monopoly power, and they have tried to exercise it in the past.[3] The available evidence suggests that it is negligible. Monopoly power exists when a firm or group of firms can charge a price consistently above that which would rule in competitive conditions and, as a consequence, reap monopoly profits and/or incur higher operating costs than they would in a competitive industry.

Parallel pricing

The Monopolies Commission has argued that in concentrated industries monopoly profits can be earned because firms will take pricing decisions with 'conscious recognition . . . of [their] . . . interdependence',[4] rather than independently in response to impersonal changes in cost or demand conditions. The sellers in the industry then follow the lead of a major supplier, or act in common. The Commission distinguishes this type of (disciplined) parallel pricing from what is called 'barometric' price leadership. Outwardly the two are similar, but the barometric leader is followed only because his pricing behaviour is taken by the others as a reliable indicator of real changes in the underlying cost and demand conditions. Professor Jesse Markham has argued that such a leader 'appears to do little more than set prices that would eventually be set by [the] forces of competition'.[5] So, where monopolistic harm results from parallel pricing, it is due not so much to the practice itself

---

[1] Part of the definition laid down by the Fair Trading Act, 1973 (Sections 3(i) and 3(ii) of the 1948 Act defined the threshold as 'one-third' or more of the supply).

[2] HC 412, paras. 457, 459, and 484-487.

[3] For example, the restrictive agreements on discounts from 1970 to 1974 (above, p. 12).

[4] Cmnd. 5330, para. 9.

[5] 'The Nature and Significance of Price Leadership', *American Economic Review*, Vol. XLI, December 1951, p. 899.

TABLE XII
COSTS AND SCALE FOR BAKERIES

Capacity of Ovens per hr. (Sacks of flour)	Approx. Potential Output per hr		Total Capital Cost	Index of Capital Costs per unit of Output	No. of Operatives	Index of Direct Costs per unit of Output
	Sacks	Index				
9/10	7½	100	100	100	11	100
18/20	18/20	240/267	160/165	77/80	18	61-68
27/30	27/30	360/400	190/200	58/61	20	45-50

Source: C. F. Pratten, *op. cit.*, p. 79.

but, according to the Polanyis, 'to the existence of monopolistic conditions which enable the more disciplined type of leadership to prevail'.[1]

There is no doubt that recommended retail prices in the bread industry have moved closely in parallel, even in periods of freedom from control. It is not so obvious that wholesale prices have moved so closely in step. There have been frequent discount wars ever since Spillers first breached the standard 12½ per cent level on the 'Wonderloaf' brand. The Commission views such activity as 'incompatible with a fully co-ordinated policy'.[2]

Moreover,

'. . . entry conditions are a crucial element in any consideration of the public interest issues raised by restrictions on competitive behaviour . . . in the case of parallel pricing'.[3]

If entry barriers are low, sellers cannot long persist in maintaining prices above a competitive level. The competitive process of entry has been seen to have worked on several occasions in the bread industry.[4] High monopoly profits or inefficiently high costs encourage new firms to enter an industry at a lower price and/or at a lower cost than in existing firms.

Table XII confirms the Monopolies Commission's view that

'the minimum efficient size of plant is small and neither it nor the capital expenditures involved is likely to present a very formidable barrier to new entry'.[5]

[1] G. and P. Polanyi, 'Parallel Pricing: A Harmful Practice?', *Moorgate and Wall Street,* Spring 1974, p. 43.

[2] Cmnd. 5330, para. 27.

[3] Cmnd. 5330, para. 70.

[4] Above, pp. 16-18.

[5] Cmnd. 5330, para. 45.

C. F. Pratten found that an optimum-sized bakery would require a 30-sack per hour output, which would provide sufficient bread for a town of 500,000 people. But what scale economies there are on capital and labour would be substantially 'damped down' by the costs of materials (only small economies are available on bulk distribution) and by diseconomies of distribution of the finished product. He calculated that a plant with the most modern techniques operating at only half this minimum efficient scale would incur at worst only a 7·5 per cent increase in total unit costs.[1]

Innovation and ease of entry

The importance of competition by innovation in the industry has been emphasised (pp. 41-43); so has the frequency of entry over the longer run. In the immediate past such pressures are still very obvious, as is the unimportance of scale as an entry barrier.

One group of likely entrants is the retail grocery chains. Safeways opened the first in-store bakery (where ingredients are mixed and baked in the supermarket, often in view of the customer) in Bedford in 1963.[2] Another group of probable entrants is the biscuit manufacturers. They possess considerable expertise in purchasing and processing flour, and also in marketing baked products through independent outlets.[3] Neither they nor large retailers are likely to be deterred by high capital costs of entry.

Moreover, smaller firms are again presenting a very real threat to the dominance of the Big Three, partly because of the gradual swing in consumer preferences away from the standard loaf towards less homogeneous commodities, partly because of changing conditions of supply. The Bread and Flour (Amendment) Regulations of 1972 permitted the use of a chemical in breadmaking (L-cysteine hydrochloride). This enables 'activated dough development' to shorten the fermentation period required by small-scale bakers, and improves their

---

[1] Pratten, *op. cit.*, p. 80. Even this may overstate the minimum efficient scale. The 1977 Monopolies Commission Report suggested that it lay as low as 12-18 sacks per hour. (HC 412, para. 104.)

[2] Maunder, *op. cit.*, p. 45.

[3] At least one biscuit manufacturer already has a financial interest in a number of milling companies. (HC 412, para. 83.)

yield per sack of flour.[1] It recaptures for the small-scale master baker many of the cost advantages gained only by firms large enough to employ the 'Chorleywood Bread Process'.[2] As a consequence, and because suitable plant can cost as little as £8,000,[3] hot-bread shops have appeared as one of the major retailing and manufacturing innovations of the 1970s.

The reality of this potential competition disciplining the industry's behaviour, together with the desire of the Big Three not to live in a collusive environment producing a homogeneous product,[4] is epitomised by ABF's recent counter-entry into the hot-bread shop trade. Since 1974 it has opened or converted some 200 shops which bake bread on the premises. The loaves produced are varied and are generally of the more traditional types. If sliced and wrapped standard bread is sold it is bought in from a 'Sunblest' bakery, often with a non-'Sunblest' wrapper. In addition to bread baking (from the raw material stage on), the shops also bake savoury goods (pre-prepared in the plants) and decorate some flour confectionery (pre-baked in the plants). None of this indicates an industry behaving monopolistically.

Trends in profits

What of profits? The figures in Table I (p. 13) indicated losses which speak more of a squeeze on costs and prices brought about by the joint action of competition and regulation than they do of monopolistic practices. The most dramatic cost increases have been in the price of wheat, due partly to world commodity price trends (like the bad Russian harvest of 1972), and partly to Britain's entry into the EEC, which has resulted in the gradual harmonisation of agricultural policies so that millers in Britain are now having to pay a much higher price for wheat (which accounts for 90 per cent of the cost of flour).

For the Big Three it probably makes little difference where they make their profit, from sales of flour to their bakery divisions, or from sales of bread to the public, provided the

[1] HC 412, para. 47.

[2] The Chorleywood Process, introduced in 1961, is highly mechanised and involves a short period of intensive mechanical working, plus the addition of an oxidising improver to the flour, and an emulsifying agent. Fermentation time is less and yield is larger than with conventional baking techniques.

[3] HC 412, para. 111.

[4] '. . . co-ordination of price policies will be strengthened where products do not differ significantly . . .' (Cmnd. 5330, para. 7.)

[63]

total return is considered satisfactory. To the extent that the independent plant and master bakers still have a role to play in the competitive process, the separation of milling from baking is of importance. They must still obtain their flour from the millers at market prices and cannot subsidise one side of their business from the profits of the other.

Thus although I contend that the monopoly power of the Big Three is of little significance, it is of growing importance because of government regulation. Government policy, in the shape of the bread subsidy and the Price Code, has weakened the competitive position of the independent bakers *vis à vis* the Big Three. The integrated groups have benefited from the mechanics of the schemes, while the independent plant bakers have suffered. The subsidy and price increases have been awarded by the so-called 'back-marker' principle, so that the amount allowed has been the lowest increase proposed by any one firm.[1] Inevitably it has been one of the integrated Big Three, and in particular ABF. The pre-notified price rises applied for by ABF, RHM and Spillers in the Parliamentary Session 1973-74, for example, were 5·27, 7·02 and 8·86 per cent respectively.[2] The price rise eventually permitted and subsidy granted would be geared to the 'back-marker' in that batch of applications, namely ABF. The 'back-marker' principle may have had the merit of rewarding the most efficient integrated milling and baking firm and penalising the less efficient, but it implicitly rests on the assumption that *integration* is the most efficient form of organisation for the industry. At best this is an unproven assumption.

Monopoly policy deleterious in bread

Monopolies legislation is frequently invoked by government when market concentration in an industry increases. Most government policy in the bread industry, however, is having the effect of strengthening the market leaders and weakening non-integrated firms. The unavoidable paradox of *increased concentration due to government legislation*[3] is the outcome—as in the advertising moratorium, the discount freeze and the relatively strict price controls imposed on bread *vis à vis* flour.

[1] HC 412, para. 228.

[2] HC 56, 1973-74.

[3] Hawley's, owned by Express Dairies, was the country's fourth largest bread baker until its closure in 1977 (*Daily Telegraph*, 18 November, 1977).

When invoked, British monopolies legislation, unlike American antitrust laws, rightly judges the situation more in terms of market conduct than of industrial structure. But in no area *untouched* by government interference do the firms in the bread market appear to be behaving in a monopolistic manner. Innovation is rife. Profitability is low or non-existent. Predatory practices such as the withholding of flour supplies from independent bakers other than at disadvantageously high prices is not possible because of the continuing existence of a large number of independent millers. And hanging over the whole industry is the persistent threat of further entry should costs rise to such inefficiently high levels that other firms, such as biscuit manufacturers or the retail multiples, might feel they could reap the profits which go with more efficiency.

By weakening the non-integrated firms the government's legislative framework is indeed reducing competition. These firms, the independent plant bakers (when they have not been debarred by legislation from practising price competition), have proved to be highly efficient, low-cost, low-price producers whom the Big Three ignored at their peril. Their advertising, physical distribution costs and overheads tend to be lower than those of the Groups. And their willingness to award higher discounts, even though within a restricted geographical region, has compelled the Groups to match their price reductions in the area. Moreover, an independent baker selling at a low price to the regional branches of a national supermarket chain often stimulates the retailer to claim matching prices nationally from the Big Three.[1,2]

(iv) *The balance of payments*

Some 2·4 million tons of wheat were imported into Britain from Manitoba, the USA, Russia and Australia in 1975.[3] 'Thishard' wheat has more protein and less starch than domestically grown 'soft' wheat. The proportions of hard to soft in white flour are approximately 60:40. It is the high proportion of hard wheat in the flour which gives the standard loaf its good keeping qualities. British bread will stay 'fresh' for several

---

[1] HC 412, para. 293.

[2] Examples of important independent bakers include Darbyshire's Prize Bread Co. of Blackpool, Fine Lady Bakeries of Banbury, and William Gunstone & Sons Ltd. of Sheffield. The Federation of Bakers has over 40 independent members.

[3] HC 412, para. 17.

days. French bread, traditionally baked entirely from soft flour, stays fresh for only a few hours and the French housewife will typically make a twice-daily purchase of bread to ensure fresh supplies. It is unlikely that the British housewife would willingly change her shopping habits so dramatically that she would emulate her French sister in order to minimise the nation's bill for flour imports. Millers and bakers have long appreciated this consumer attitude, and both before and during the current changeover to the EEC pricing rules for agricultural produce have been willing to pay a higher price for hard wheat.[1]

The old criticism that the British plant bread manufacturing and distribution system does not permit the housewife to exercise her choice in this way is, of course, a fallacy. The continuing existence of master bakers, in-store bakeries, and now hot-bread shops provides the necessary framework for the market to swing towards French-style bread if consumer preferences so demand it. In the meantime some millers, such as Rank, have voluntarily paid a higher price to British farmers to encourage them to grow certain varieties of soft wheat which produce acceptable results in a 50:50 rather than a 60:40 blend of flour.[2] In other words, the market has reacted precisely in the way micro-economic theory would suggest, and so long as imported wheat is more expensive than domestic this open market reaction can be expected to continue, provided only that the industry produces a loaf which meets the consumer's preferences at a price she is willing to pay.

No good economic reason to restrict imports

Other than the perennial British preoccupation with the balance of payments, there seems no reason why discriminatory measures should be taken against a product the market clearly prefers. The general arguments against quotas or tariffs on imported wheat, of course, also apply. Any such action reduces world wealth by attracting resources to uses which are not their potentially most productive (as valued by the market). The only really convincing argument for control of wheat imports is that the nation should be self-sufficient in food

---

[1] £32 instead of £27 per ton in 1970. (*Sunday Times,* 4 December, 1970.) By 1977 North American wheat, at £116 per ton, was £28 per ton more expensive than EEC wheat.

[2] *Sunday Times, ibid.*

supplies, and in particular bread, for defensive and strategic reasons. Even that argument loses much of its conviction when it is considered that, even if a conventional war was fought, bread forms only a small proportion of our diet. Professor (Lord) Robbins long ago rightly indicated that national security may be much more cheaply guaranteed by protecting lines of communications and building stocks of basic food-stuffs.[1] This is probably still true.

(v) *Industry rationalisation*

The argument of the NBPI for further concentration of production on the standard loaf (p. 32) seemed to have the objective of lowering unit costs irrespective of consumer preferences. In addition, it discovered that selling and delivery expenses (excluding discounts) came to 24 per cent of total costs.[2]

It arrived at the following conclusions:

'Commonsense would suggest that special services such as van delivery to the door should be separately charged for . . . in practice, a penny is added to the price of a loaf in some areas . . . this differential does not, in many cases, fully reflect the difference in cost as between selling bread at the doorstep and selling it in the shop. . . . We consider that . . . a baker . . . should specify a service charge fully reflecting [this] extra cost. . . A quicker reduction still might be effected if manufacturers could agree on an apportionment of streets . . . instead of their trundling their vans competitively up and down the same streets.'[3]

Whatever political or administrative 'commonsense' is or might say about charging separate prices for delivery, economic theory asserts that a separate charge will be made only if the marginal benefit obtained from making the charge exceeds the marginal costs of collecting it. The marginal costs of identifying market segments with different elasticities of demand and so differing willingnesses to pay a separate charge can be high. The identification of a group of consumers who would willingly pay a premium of 1p per loaf from those who would pay either a ½p or 2p differential requires substantial market knowledge. The acquisition of such knowledge is not costless; it requires either expensive market research and/or the risk of costly loss

---

[1] *Economic Planning and International Order,* Macmillan, 1937, p. 310.

[2] Cmnd. 4329, para. 9.

[3] Cmnd. 2760, paras. 46-7.

of custom if errors of judgement are made. As a consequence, it is generally more efficient in use of resources to categorise groupings in the market-place broadly and charge them appropriate prices rather than attempt to identify each individual consumer's willingness to pay a price 'fully reflecting the extra cost' of a van travelling 100 yards, 200 yards or 300 yards. In brief, the possible economy is trivial and it would be costly to obtain, so that the net saving would be nothing—or worse.

The NBPI (in the footsteps of the Food Council of the 1920s and 1930s) ran true to form in their disparaging dismissal of competition. The vans 'trundling competitively' up and down the same street contain whole ranges of foods other than bread. To the extent that they contain bread the ranges are not restricted to the standard loaf. They include speciality breads, high-bran breads, fancy loaves, and so on. It is, as noted, precisely the dynamic process of competition which has resulted in this width of consumer choice. The vans do *not* contain the same merchandise *because* they 'trundle competitively' side by side: if there was one van in each 'apportioned' street (by the objectionable monopolistic device of market sharing) it would contain a narrower range and the housewife would not be able to buy the bread she wanted.

Investment depends on raising rate of profit

In production, rationalisation has been slower than might have been expected from the merger movement of the 1950s and 1960s. It was generally 'cheaper in private and social terms to continue baking in the old (fully depreciated but still functioning) ovens'.[1] Old plants tended not to be closed until repair costs rose sufficiently to tip the investment decision in favour of replacement. This sensible investment policy has now reached the stage where investment in new plant is highly desirable. The rate of return from bread-baking is now so low, however, that relatively little investment is being undertaken. The statement by the chairman of RHM that he 'will shut his bakeries until he can find someone prepared to run them at a loss'[2] was possibly melodramatic. But in so far as regulatory action is desirable to further the rationalisation and modernisation of the industry, it should take the form of the removal rather than the addition of controls.

[1] Hart, Utton and Walshe, *op. cit.,* p. 51.
[2] *Financial Times,* 28 March, 1973.

Provided the incentive of profits is present to encourage investment, the industry should be well placed to take advantage of the increasing private ownership of deep freezes. In 1966 24 per cent of bread production took place on a Friday.[1] This had not altered by 1977.[2] Such a violently fluctuating pattern of demand inevitably results in a good deal of labour-force slack in midweek, and working overtime at weekends. This arrangement does not represent under-utilisation of capacity, rather the provision of adequate capacity to meet fluctuating market demand. Nonetheless, it is possible to change these consumption patterns. The advent of deep-freeze storage in the home could enable the industry to use its plant and labour force more efficiently.[3] The industry has the opportunity to cut costs and raise profits, by encouraging housewives, through advertising, to use bread as a deep-freeze space-filler (and so also minimise their shopping effort). But the incentive of profitability must be allowed by government to encourage the industry to act accordingly. It has been said by the Prime Minister of industry generally:

'The willingness of industry to invest in new plant and machinery requires . . . that industry is left with sufficient funds and sufficient confidence to make the new investment . . . I mean they must be able to earn a surplus which is a euphemism for saying that they must make a profit.'[4]

VI. CONCLUSIONS AND RECOMMENDATIONS

A. SUMMARY AND CONCLUSIONS

The conclusions of this study can be summarised as follows:

1. Bread is baked in an old-established industry experiencing a long-term secular decline in demand.

2. The industry has been subject to almost uninterrupted government regulation for seven centuries.

3. The concentration of ownership in the industry is not reflected in the diffusion of manufacturing capacity.

---

[1] Cmnd. 4428, para. 13.

[2] HC 412, para. 103.

[3] In 1971, 3 per cent of households owned a deep freeze; by 1976 the proportion had risen to 16 per cent. (Information supplied by Audits of Great Britain Ltd.)

[4] Mr James Callaghan, at the Labour Party Conference, 28 September, 1976.

4. Economies of scale are of minor importance when the output of a plant is homogeneous. When output is heterogeneous consumers willingly offset any cost increase by paying producers a 'premium' price.

5. The history of the industry is mostly one of government-supported (or government-initiated) monopoly or cartel, which has thwarted the competitive process but has ultimately broken down as new methods of satisfying consumer demand for bread have arisen.

(a) The Assize of Bread and the London Bakers' Company kept bread prices higher in the capital than they were in the provinces, obstructed competition by provincial bakers in the City, and protected inefficient producers.

(b) The Food Council's price recommendations made in agreement with the National Association of Master Bakers between the mid-1920s and 1939 kept prices high where the NAMB was strong and inhibited new entry.

(c) Small town and village monopolies were broken by the entry of plants selling to a wide geographical area through non-conventional outlets.

(d) Price control and subsidy schemes from 1941-56 reduced or prevented price, product and promotional competition. The schemes were operated by the government in association with the Federation of Wholesale and Multiple Bakers and resulted in smaller bakers being driven from the industry irrespective of their efficiency or ability to provide the consumer with a product she wanted at a price she was prepared to pay.

(e) The market power of millers and plant bakers respectively has tended to be curbed by the backward integration of retail bakers such as Allied or retail sellers of bread such as Lyons or Safeways.

(f) The various price controls since 1965 have strengthened the position of the fully integrated baking and milling firms who can cross-subsidise less profitable activities (price-restricted bread baking) from more profitable (milling): in consequence the competitive potential of the independent plants and of the master bakers has been seriously weakened.

(g) Government agencies such as the National Board for

Prices and Incomes have recommended and encouraged product standardisation and distribution rationalisation which benefits larger firms at the expense of smaller and encourages product homogeneity. Consumer choice is narrowed. Explicit collusion is thus permitted, and focal points for tacit collusion created. Consumer benefits from an increase in competitive behaviour and a reduction of monopoly power are reduced.

(h) The 1974 bread subsidy scheme, its dependence on the close co-operation of the Big Three, the Price Commission and the Department of Prices and Consumer Protection, has been the natural outgrowth of the NBPI recommendations. It has been restricted to some types of bread, so benefiting the large-scale specialised producer, weakening the more generalist manufacturer, and thus making the industry as a whole less responsive to consumer demand.

(i) The 1975-76 advertising moratorium 'trade-off' with a freeze on discounts negotiated semi-formally between the Big Three and the DPCP weakened the competitive potential of independent plants consequently no longer permitted to compete by price.

(j) The 1974 discount freeze resulted in a diminution of countervailing power. Retailers were restricted in the degree to which they could compete by price. In some retailers (the multiples) bread prices probably rose, in others (the voluntary groups) prices paid by consumers certainly rose.

(k) The discount freeze also minimised the incentives to grocers to purchase from only one source of supply and so minimise the industry's transport costs.

(l) The ability of multiple retailers to collude tacitly and refrain from price competition was buttressed by the combination of the discount freeze and the gross margin controls of the Price Code.

6. When the limitations on discounting were removed by the government they were effectively reimposed by the delivery men's trade union.

7. When controls (imposed by government or trade union) were not present the industry engaged in fierce competition *via* price, product, promotion and place at all stages (Big

Three, independent plant, master baker and independent multiple retailer).

8. Government regulation of the bread industry cannot be justified on welfare, defence, balance-of-payments or technological grounds.

9. The invocation of the legislation of 1958 and 1964 on restrictive practices encouraged and facilitated price competition in the industry.

10. The industry is becoming more integrated. Partly this may have been due to market forces; it has certainly been partly due to the legislative environment which has hampered the survival prospects of independent bakers. The Monopolies Commission accepted (and gave no evidence why it did so) the views of the Big Three that vertical integration results in cost savings.[1] It also accepted, again without apparent proof, that independent bakers can 'enjoy certain cost advantages'.[2] These contrary opinions suggest that there is no obvious and conclusive reason why the industry would (or would not) be more efficiently organised on a vertically-integrated basis. When government prevents competition by setting a price floor (as with the discount freeze) it will take place in other dimensions. Further vertical integration has been one such response by firms which had the appropriate resources and expertise. This may or may not be the industrial structure preferred by the market.

B. RECOMMENDATIONS FOR POLICY

Given these conclusions, given the objective (consumer protection through competition) of the Fair Trading Act, 1973, what policy recommendations can be made?

1. All government price controls, subsidies and recommended price discount structures should be removed. They have distorted the structure, conduct and performance of the industry.

2. The only objective test available to indicate which form of industrial organisation is the most appropriate for meeting

[1] HC 412, paras. 491-2.
[2] HC 412, para. 293.

consumer demands is the market itself.[1] The Monopolies Commission's complacent acceptance of a loss-making bread industry, which implies cross-subsidisation, should be rejected. If the current structure is the most appropriate, the burden of proof lies on those who make that assertion. In the absence of controls, cross-subsidisation and monopolistic practices, the evolution of an integrated industry would be self-evident proof of comparative efficiency. Such a market test should be made; even if imperfect it would be superior to the alternative of political judgement.

3. Explicit acceptance of flour milling as a relatively high-return industry and baking as a relatively low-return one is wrong. More important is the need to ensure that profits are neither monopolistically inflated nor artificially depressed. Competition policy should be geared to ensure that there are no impediments to the free movement of capital into milling and out of baking.

4. Regulation should not favour one sector of industry at the expense of another: milling v. baking, baking v. retailing, or sub-sectors such as multiples v. voluntary groups.

5. The imposition of a restraint of trade by the United Road Transport Union on the bakers and retailers should be regarded as a restrictive trade practice by the Office of Fair Trading. Provision exists (for example in Sections 13 and 14 of the Fair Trading Act) to enable the OFT to refer the action of the union to the Consumer Protection Advisory Committee as 'a consumer trade practice' which 'adversely affects the economic interests of consumers'.

6. Legislation requiring date-of-sale (or -consumption) labelling should be introduced so that consumers can identify the relative freshness of wrapped bread.

7. Government officials (Ministers and civil servants) should cease referring to the 'standard loaf'. By use and wont, backed by the Weights and Measures Acts, this term has encouraged the industry to produce a homogeneous product, which in turn has encouraged and facilitated cartel-like behaviour.

8. The 1973 Fair Trading Act should be broadened to enable the Monopolies Commission to appraise the impact on

---

[1] This assumes that monopoly itself is absent, that there are no externalities or inequities, and that other criteria are met. (Above, pp. 56-69.)

competition of government-inspired or government-condoned restrictions on an industry's competitive behaviour. The Commission should examine not only price competition but also non-price competition. The Commission's investigation into bread revealed unsuccessful price collusion which was observed with 'regret'. But very successful banning of advertising and freezing of discounts (both with government approval) was also discovered. They passed unremarked by the Commission despite their damaging impact on competition and on the final price consumers had to pay. Despite the contents of elementary economics textbooks (and some advanced ones),[1] effective competition is not restricted to the one dimension of price.

In general, therefore, the recent Monopolies Commission investigation was not carried out within an interpretation of the 1948 Act and according to the guidelines of current competition policy (the 1973 Act). More specifically, the above recommendations would make the market for bread more competitive. Consumers would have more power to exercise their choice in purchasing bread of the quantity and quality they desire at the price they are prepared to pay. Bread firms would be further compelled to be efficient in satisfying consumer wants. The really startling conclusion is that, after long exposure to stringent controls, the profit-maximising motivation of business men has continued to serve the consumer interest by providing lower prices, variety of products, cheaper processes and new sources of supply. Somnolent colluders have always been displaced by thrusting entrepreneurs for the benefit of both consumer and entrepreneur. Only when the collusion has been bolstered by government has the competitive process worked more sluggishly than it otherwise would have.

[1] The Open University Set Book, *Introduction to Economic Analysis*, by Miles Fleming, George Allen and Unwin, 1969, states (p. 196) that 'non-price competition . . . must be left for more advanced study'. But Donald Dewey's more advanced text, *Microeconomics*, Oxford, 1975, contains no discussion of non-price competition. Yet in a *footnote* (p. 253) the following critical remarks appear: '. . . economic policy ought to aim at creating the conditions necessary for the kind of dynamic competition that brings about the right kinds of economic progress. And this goal . . . is incompatible with making (price) competition as perfect as possible.' Mr Dewey then refers the reader to J. M. Clark, *Competition as a Dynamic Process*, The Brookings Institution, Washington DC, 1961. Clark emphasises 'effective' as 'workable' competition, and includes place, product and promotion, as well as price, in his definition.

QUESTIONS FOR DISCUSSION

1. Why is a low price for bread a desirable objective? When is it undesirable?

2. Explain why a collusively high price for a product cannot persist without government enforcement. Apply the analysis to the bread industry.

3. Is rivalry by price the ultimate yardstick to judge whether or not an industry is effectively competitive? Is bread an exception?

4. Attempt a discussion of the reasons why ABF entered the hot-bread shop market:
    i. to guarantee outlets for flour?
    ii. to strengthen its position as a supplier of standard bread?
    iii. to meet consumer preferences?
    iv. to sell products not subject to price controls?
    v. to improve profitability?

5. Are iii. and v. mutually exclusive?

6. Why did government controls result in higher bread prices in the 19th century, the 1920s-40s, and the 1970s?

7. Has product quality suffered or improved as a result of government control of the bread industry?

8. Which of the following do not exercise pricing discipline on the activities of the Big Three:
    i. master bakers
    ii. independent plant bakers
    iii. independent millers
    iv. multiple retailers
    v. independent retail grocers
    vi. biscuit manufacturers
    vii. housewives
    viii. government
    ix. hot-bread shops
    x. the United Road Transport Union?

9. In the absence of government controls, why would an industry theoretically become vertically integrated? Does bread differ from other industries?

10. What evidence is there that the conditions in answer to question 9 exist in milling and baking? What evidence is there that they do not exist? Which set of evidence is the stronger?

FURTHER READING

Baird, Charles W., *Prices and Markets*, West, 1975 (especially pp. 145-50).

Brozen, Yale, *The Competitive Economy*, General Learning Press, 1974.

Hart, P. E., Utton, M.A., and Walshe, G., *Mergers and Concentration in British Industry*, Cambridge University Press, 1973.

Hindley, Brian, *Industrial Merger and Public Policy*, Hobart Paper No. 50, Institute of Economic Affairs, 1970.

Kirzner, Israel, *Competition and Entrepreneurship*, University of Chicago Press, 1973.

Markham, Jesse W., 'The Nature and Significance of Price Leadership', *American Economic Review*, Vol. 41, December 1951.

Maunder, W. P. J., 'Price Leadership: An Appraisal of its Character in Some British Industries', *The Business Economist*, Vol. iv, No. 3, Autumn 1972.

Mises, Ludwig von, *Human Action*, 3rd Edition, Henry Regnery, Chicago, 1966 (especially Chapters XV and XVI).

Pickering, J. F., *Industrial Structure and Market Conduct*, Martin Robertson, London, 1974.

Polanyi, George, *Which Way Monopoly Policy?*, Research Monograph No. 30, Institute of Economic Affairs, London, 1973.

Pratten, C. F., *Economies of Scale in Manufacturing Industry*, Cambridge University Press, 1971.

Rowley, Charles K. (ed.), *Readings in Industrial Economics*, Macmillan, 1972.

Scherer, F. M., *Industrial Pricing*, Rand McNally, 1970.

Sherman, Roger, *The Economics of Industry*, Little, Brown & Co., Boston, 1974.

Stigler, George J., *The Theory of Price*, 3rd Edition, Macmillan, London, 1966 (especially Chapter 13, 'Cartels and Mergers').

Stigler, George J., *The Organisation of Industry*, Richard D. Irwin, 1968.

Swann, D., O'Brien, D. P., Maunder, W. P. J. and Howe, W. S., *Competition in British Industry*, George Allen and Unwin, London, 1974.

Worcester, D. A., 'Why "Dominant Firms" Decline', *Journal of Political Economy*, Vol. 65, August 1957.

Yamey, Basil S. (ed.), *Economics of Industrial Structure*, Penguin Books, Harmondsworth, Middlesex, 1973.